Life Annuity Products and Their Guarantees

Please cite this publication as:
OECD (2016), *Life Annuity Products and Their Guarantees*, OECD Publishing, Paris.
http://dx.doi.org/10.1787/9789264265318-en

ISBN 978-92-64-26530-1 (print)
ISBN 978-92-64-26531-8 (PDF)

Photo credits: © Ekachai Lohacamonchai/iStock/Thinkstock.com.

Corrigenda to OECD publications may be found on line at: *www.oecd.org/publishing/corrigenda*.

Foreword

This publication presents the work of the OECD project on annuity products and their guarantees. The project seeks to better understand the types of products available, the guarantees that they offer, and how policy can support the role of these products in financing retirement.

The first chapter describes the criteria that define the scope of the discussion around annuity products for retirement. It provides a classification of the different types of annuity products in order to establish a common language with which to discuss annuity products and markets. The second chapter provides an overview of the specific types of annuity products available, as well as the markets in which they can be found. The third chapter focuses on the risks that these products present to annuity providers and how they are managed, describing product features and risk management strategies for each product in depth. The fourth chapter discusses some considerations relating to drivers of annuity product design, availability, and sustainability as well as the potential role of regulation, relying on examples found in various markets to guide the discussion. The fifth chapter considers consumer protection issues relating to annuity products, in particular how these products are communicated and distributed to individuals. Chapter 6 discusses the challenges that policy makers face in incorporating annuity products into the retirement landscape and presents the key policy considerations with respect to the issues raised.

The project on annuity products and their guarantees is part of the research and policy programme of work of the OECD Insurance and Private Pension Committee (IPPC) and, in particular, its Working Party on Private Pensions (WPPP). The WPPP is an international body that brings together policy makers, regulators and the private sector from all OECD countries to discuss issues related to the operation and regulation of funded retirement income systems.

This publication was prepared by Pablo Antolin and Jessica Mosher of the Financial Affairs Division of the OECD Directorate for Financial and Enterprise Affairs. It has greatly benefited from the comments of national government delegates of the IPPC and the WPPP, as well as representatives of industry bodies. We would especially like to thank Manuel Aguilera, previous Chair of the IPPC, and Ambrogio Rinaldi, Chair of the WPPP, for their useful advice, support and valuable inputs to this project. Editorial and communication support was provided by Pauline Arbel, Pamela Duffin, Kate Lancaster and Edward Smiley.

The OECD gratefully acknowledges the financial support from Prudential Financial to the OECD work on private pensions.

Table of contents

Tables

Figures

Executive summary

As a result of the shifting retirement landscape, individuals are bearing increasing responsibility to manage the financing of their own retirement, not only in the saving and investment decisions they make during the accumulation of assets but also how they will draw down their assets in retirement. Along with this increased responsibility comes increased risk, both in terms of the investment risk of lower investment returns than expected, but especially the longevity risk of outliving assets in retirement.

Annuity products can provide guarantees which protect individuals from such risks, providing minimum guaranteed returns, guaranteed income and/or protection against longevity risk. Policy makers therefore have a strong interest to better understand the products and guarantees which are available in order to assess the potential role of these products in mitigating these risks for individuals as well as to put in place a framework to encourage the development of these products and ensure their sustainability.

In this context, the primary goal of the OECD project on Annuity Products presented in this publication is to better understand annuity products and the guarantees they provide. Product design is a crucial factor in the potential role of annuity products within the pension system, the cost and demand for these products, and the resulting risks that are borne by the annuity providers. Increasingly complex products, however, pose additional challenges with respect to consumer protection. Consumers need to be aware of their options and have access to unbiased and comprehensible advice and information for these products. Policy makers must have an understanding of these issues in order to ensure that annuity products can be optimally used as part of the solution to finance retirement and that these products remain sustainable for the annuity provider and suitable for consumers.

Key findings and conclusions

Annuity product features and design

- There is a need for more consistency in the definitions and terminology used to discuss the role of annuity products in financing retirement, as the lack of a common language currently leads to a lack of comparability of annuity products and markets across jurisdictions.
- The annuity products available can be grouped into three main types of products: those offering fixed payments which are defined in advance, those offering payments which are indexed to an objective measure which varies over time, and those which function as retirement savings products but that also offer the option for the consumer to convert the accumulated assets into a guaranteed income stream at retirement.

- There is a trade-off between flexibility, protection and cost; increased flexibility increases the cost of annuity products, while reduced protection and increased risk sharing will lower the cost.

Coherence in the design of the pension framework

- The rules relating to the accumulation and drawdown of pensions should accommodate the use of annuity products.
- Any limits on product design should be in the consumer's and/or annuity provider's best interest and should not unduly increase the risk exposure or cost of the product.
- Limits on market segmentation for annuities should not exclude certain populations from the annuity market.

Encouragement of the demand for annuity products

- Any mandate for the purchase of an annuity should consider the heterogeneous needs of different segments of society.
- Any default provision of annuities should be carefully designed in order to make sure that there are still competitive pressures on annuity providers.
- The provision of information on annuity products and options available should effectively engage consumers in the decision to purchase an annuity.
- Providing fiscal incentives for annuity products can encourage demand.

Ensuring the sustainability of annuity products

- Approaches based on principles to determine capital requirements are better able than static requirements to adapt to changing product features and risks coming from product innovations and increased product complexity.
- The appropriate risk management of annuity products by providers should be encouraged through the monitoring of appropriate accounting measures, the allowance of effective risk mitigating actions and the recognition of risk-reducing measures in the capital requirements.

Ensuring the suitability of annuity products for consumers

- Product disclosures need to simply and effectively communicate product features, risks and costs.
- Increased product complexity may also lead to an increased need for financial advice, and policy makers need to ensure that advisors are knowledgeable and qualified and that the advice provided is suitable for consumers.

Chapter 1

What is an annuity product?

This chapter presents the scope and the definition of the annuity products discussed in this publication. It also proposes a classification for the various types of annuity products available to finance retirement.

The definition of an annuity product at first glance seems simple. It is a product which offers a stream of income payments to be paid to the individual. Nevertheless the literature and discussion of annuities, annuity income, and annuity markets is fraught with misunderstanding and a lack of comparability. 'Annuity income' is commonly used to refer not only to income received from annuity products, but to employer provided defined benefit pensions, or even to the income that individuals receive from public pensions. Data provided on the size of annuity markets with the purpose of demonstrating the relative role of these products in providing income in retirement may include data on 'annuity products' from which no income is expected to be received, or alternatively for which no income is guaranteed. Even terminology used to label certain types annuity products can be applied to two different products which bear no resemblance to one another.

In order to be able to begin an analysis and discussion of annuity products, we must first come to an agreement on what exactly is being discussed. First, the aim of the discussion on annuity products here is to better understand how they can fit into the retirement landscape, therefore the focus is on annuities whose primary purpose is to provide income in retirement. As such, annuities providing income due to disability or to cover healthcare costs are not considered here. While these additional guarantees covering health issues can be embedded in the types of products discussed here, the scope of this discussion does not cover the associated product designs and risks of these types of products.

Beyond the scope of products providing income in retirement, a more precise definition needs to be laid out in order to distinguish between vehicles providing 'annuity income', products which may be commonly referred to as annuities but do not actually function as such, and products which actually provide no guarantees at all. While public pensions and defined benefit plans can provide annuity income, they should not be in the scope of the discussion on annuity products here. Similarly products referred to as 'annuities' but that never result in a guaranteed income being paid should be excluded. Finally, while drawdown products providing structure to the payout phase could also potentially play an important role in the evolving retirement landscape, they are not the focus of the discussion here as no longevity guarantees are generally provided.

Coming to an agreement on the definition and classification annuity products will provide the foundation on which annuity products can be discussed and their features, guarantees and market size compared across jurisdictions. With this aim, this chapter first puts forward a set of criteria on which to base the definition of an annuity product for the discussion presented here, and justifies this definition based on concrete examples from different jurisdictions. Based on these criteria, a classification of different categories and types of annuity products is then proposed to provide a foundation for defining a common language with which to subsequently base the discussion of annuity markets, products and their guarantees contained in this publication.

Criteria to define an annuity product

The criteria presented here seek to provide answers to the questions raised regarding the features which are necessary to qualify any given income stream or product as an annuity product, given that the scope of this publication is to discuss annuity products as a solution to provide guaranteed income in retirement. These criteria are meant to be exhaustive, and each criterion will be clarified and discussed in turn.

1. An annuity product is fully financed by the contributions or premiums towards its purchase.
2. Payments are calculated on an actuarially fair basis.
3. The provider of the annuity product is the entity which promises payments to the individual or member.
4. The employer is not the guarantor of the promised payments.
5. There is a longevity insurance component in the promised payments.
6. Where receiving a future income stream from a deferred annuity is optional, the annuity conversion rate is defined at the onset of the contract.
7. Where receiving a future income stream from a deferred annuity is mandatory, the provision of the future income is established in the same contract that was established for the accumulation of the assets.

Defining the scope of what types of income streams are considered to be annuity products

An annuity product is fully financed by the contributions or premiums towards its purchase

The first criterion is that an annuity product should be fully financed by the contributions or premiums towards its purchase. This criterion in part addresses the distinction between what is considered annuity income and what is considered to be an annuity product. A product which is fully financed by contributions would generally require that premiums or contributions are put aside to fund the reserves which back the expected future annuity payments. This criterion therefore excludes PAYG pension schemes from the scope, as contributions go to fund current pensions rather than being saved to fund the future payments being promised.

Payments are calculated on an actuarially fair basis

The criterion that payments are calculated on an actuarially fair basis further clarifies the distinction between annuity income and an annuity product. Calculating payments on an actuarially fair basis means that the promised payments are computed based on a discount rate and mortality assumptions which reasonably reflect conditions at the time the annuity is purchased. This implies a direct link between contributions/premiums paid towards the annuity and the actual level of income received. Defined benefit schemes would therefore be excluded as there is not a direct link between contributions made and the promised payment.

The provider of the annuity product is the entity which promises payments to the individual or member

Requiring that the provider of the annuity product directly guarantees the income promised to the individual or member intends to make the distinction between annuities directly providing an income guarantee to the primary recipient and those purchased to reinsure income guarantees for the primary recipients. While an important topic in itself, annuity products used for de-risking other pension or annuity promises are not within the scope of the discussion here, which focuses on annuity products providing retirement income to individuals.

As such, buy-in deals common in the UK, where a pension plan purchases a bulk annuity from insurer or reinsurer to partially or totally insure its pension obligations, are not within scope. Similarly, reinsurance purchased to cover an insurer's annuity portfolio is not in scope either. These are explicit de-risking tools for entities rather than retirement solutions for the payout phase for individuals.

On the other hand, products like group annuities purchased by employers (e.g. as in Denmark) in which the promised payment is made directly by the pension fund or the insurance company are different from those examples in which the promises are reinsured by a third party, and would therefore qualify as an annuity product.

The employer is not the guarantor of the promised payments

A final criterion clarifying the scope is that the employer is not the guarantor of annuity payments. This may not be the case for specific employer provided pensions.

For example, any employer provided pensions which are kept on a book reserve basis would not be in scope as the employer has the liabilities on its balance sheet and guarantees the payments. While these types of arrangements can play an important role in the design of the payout phase, they are out of scope of the discussion put forward here.

Defining the types of products that are considered to be annuity products

A longevity insurance component is involved with the promised payments

Requiring that a longevity insurance component is involved with the promised payments delineates the difference between an annuity product and other drawdown products which can provide structure for the pay-out phase. An annuity product must provide some kind of longevity insurance guarantee to the individual guaranteeing payments for life.

There is no insurance component in the case of programmed withdrawals, as even though regular payments are provided, individuals runs the risk of depleting their fund before anticipated. Insurance wrappers for programmed withdrawals, however, could provide that insurance component. This includes the Guaranteed Lifetime Withdrawal Benefit offered with variable annuity products, which guarantees a minimum income if funds are depleted. Annuities whose payments can vary but which guarantee a minimum income level or income for life would also be considered to have an insurance component.

While term annuities guaranteeing a certain level of income for a fixed period of time, not for life, could also be considered to be annuities, these types of products are analogous to bond instruments and will not be the focus of the discussion on annuity products here.

Where receiving a future income stream from a deferred annuity is optional, the annuity conversion rate is defined at the onset of the contract

A distinction must also be made between pension savings contracts and annuity products. The first criterion to make this distinction is requiring that where receiving a future income stream from a deferred annuity is optional, the annuity conversion rate is defined at the onset of the contract. A key component in the definition of an annuity is the provision of a stream of payments. However some products may never result in a stream of payments being made if the conversion of accumulated assets into a stream of income at some point in the future is optional and the assets can be taken as a lump sum.

The variable annuity products popular in the United States provide an example of such a product. This product is a retirement savings product offering a guaranteed income option at retirement, and accumulated funds may be taken as a lump sum rather than annuitised, meaning that individuals may never receive an income stream from this product. However, these products provide a guaranteed annuity conversion rate at the time of purchase, so individuals know the minimum level of future income they could expect to receive given the level of contributions being accumulated. As the annuity conversion rate used to convert the accumulated assets into an income stream is known in advance, these products would qualify as annuity products.

An example which would not meet this criterion is the group insurance pensions which are commonly arranged by employers in Belgium. Assets are accumulated in these products with a guaranteed minimum rate of return and may be paid out as either a lump sum or an annuity, although the lump sum payment is chosen by the majority of individuals. In this case the annuity conversion rate is not defined in advance and is determined at the time the individual chooses to annuitise his assets. This type of plan could therefore be viewed as a retirement savings plan only, with an immediate annuity being purchased at retirement only if the annuity option is chosen.

Where receiving a future income stream from a deferred annuity is mandatory, the provision of the future income is established in the same contract that was established for the accumulation of the assets

This criterion further clarifies the distinction between an annuity product and a pension savings product by requiring for deferred products where taking a future income is mandatory that the provision of this income must be established in the same initial contract. Where the contract is the same, the annuity product can be considered to be purchased at the onset of the accumulation period. Where the contract is different, the annuity would begin at the time of the contract with the provider of the annuity payments.

An example to demonstrate when this criterion does not hold is the defined contribution plans in the UK, where previously 75% of accumulated assets were effectively required to be annuitized upon retirement.[1] Annuity quotes are most often given based on the amount of accumulated assets at retirement, and individuals may remain with the provider involved in the asset accumulation or choose a different annuity provider who may be offering a better price. Therefore the contract to receive annuity payments is separate from that to accumulate the assets and the provider of the annuity payments can also be different. Similar to the Belgian plans described above, these can therefore generally be viewed as retirement savings with an immediate annuity being purchased with the accumulated assets at retirement.[2]

An example where this criterion does hold would be for Riester annuity products in Germany, where a portion of the accumulated assets are required to be taken as an annuity in retirement. While the individual retains the right to change providers during the accumulation phase, the provider they are with at retirement is foreseen to be the one to provide the annuity payments. Therefore the contract with the provider includes the provision for a future income stream, qualifying these products as annuities.

The criteria outlined above provide the foundation for a common language with which to have a discussion of annuity markets and the products and guarantees offered across jurisdictions. The following section provides additional details on the different types of features and guarantees which annuity products can offer, as well as presents a framework to classify the different types of products available. This framework should then facilitate the comparison of different products across jurisdictions with respect to their features and guarantees, the risks the various products present and how these risks are managed.

Structure and features of annuity products

The plain vanilla, traditional annuity product provides guaranteed regular payments to an individual in exchange for a non-refundable upfront premium. This product thereby guarantees a stable income to the individual and protects them from the risk of outliving their assets in retirement. This basic annuity structure, however, can vary along several dimensions: the timing of the payments, the timing of the premiums, and whether the product is sold at an individual or group level.

Annuity products can either be immediate, with payments beginning right after the premium is paid, or deferred, with payments beginning at some future point in time. Immediate annuities tend to be bought with assets accumulated at retirement to provide payments through retirement. Deferred annuities are generally bought at younger ages to provide payments once the individual is retired, though may also be bought at retirement to provide old age longevity insurance and ensure that the individual will have an income if they live longer than expected.

The premiums for annuity products can be paid all at once, in a single premium, or divided into regular premium payments. Single premiums are typical for immediate annuity products, while regular premium payments are more common for deferred products, allowing individuals to contribute over time and build up the level of future income, somewhat similar to other retirement savings products.

Finally annuity products may be purchased at an individual retail level or for a group of individuals. Individual annuities are more commonly purchased by individuals within personal defined contribution pension schemes, for example, or other voluntary personal pension arrangements. Group annuities, on the other hand, are more commonly arranged by employers for a group of their employees.

Beyond the basic structures outlined above, annuity products can offer various different guarantees for the individual annuitants. These guarantees can insure the individual against several risks, namely longevity, death, investment and/or the loss of purchasing power.

The insurance against longevity risk is the risk most commonly associated with annuity products, as annuity products which provide payments for the lifetime of the individual insure against the longevity risk of outliving their assets in retirement.

Annuity products may also offer a guaranteed payment to the surviving beneficiaries of an annuitant in the case of death. This can take the form of a lump-sum payout contingent on the death of the annuitant, the provision for a lifetime payment to the surviving spouse, or the provision of a guaranteed period during which payments continue for the specified number of years regardless of the survival of the annuitant.

Investment guarantees are also common guarantees provided by annuity products, either implicitly through the guarantee of a specified level of income or explicitly through a guaranteed minimum return on the assets underlying the annuity product. These types of guarantees provide insurance against the investment risk of a decrease in asset value which could significantly reduce the level of assets available for financing retirement.

Annuities can also provide protection against the loss of purchasing power from inflation by indexing the guaranteed payments to the inflation rate, guaranteeing a level of income in real terms rather than nominal terms.

In addition to guarantees, annuity products can also offer varying levels of flexibility to the consumer, providing options with respect to the access to underlying assets and the timing and/or level of payments. For the traditional annuity product, the consumer completely relinquishes the premium assets to the annuity provider, and has no ability to get out of the contract or change the terms on which the income will be received. Variations on this traditional product, however, can offer additional flexibilities to the consumer such as control over investment decisions, the ability to withdraw from or surrender the product, or the ability to vary the level of income received during the payout phase.

Annuity providers around the world have come up with numerous variations on the traditional level fixed payment annuity product in an attempt to meet the needs of consumers and address some of the obstacles relating to the lack of demand for annuity products. The traditional annuity product is often cited as a difficult sale due in part to the lack of flexibility, particularly with respect to the access to capital and the locking-in of an investment return which could potentially increase in the future. Providers have increasingly sought to respond to these concerns through features which allow participation in market returns or company profits, access to underlying capital, and increased flexibility around the timing and design of the payout phase. At the same time, products are being designed which limit the risk to providers via risk-sharing features which reduce the levels of protection offered from the product guarantees in order to lower the cost for the consumer and better ensure the sustainability of the products for the provider.

Given the criteria and features put forward to describe an annuity product, the types of products available can be broadly classified into three product-type groups:

- The first group, **fixed payment annuities**, represents annuities for which payments are fixed and defined in advance.
- The second group of products, **indexed payment annuities**, provides annuity payments which are not known in advance and depend on the evolution of some external measure.
- The third group of products, **retirement savings with a guaranteed income option**, is characterised by the flexibility that the products offer to the consumer, particularly with respect to the access to the underlying capital. These products also commonly offer explicit guarantees to the individual during both the accumulation and payout phase.

Table 1.1 presents a classification of the main types of annuity products, grouping them into the three categories described above. The guarantees provided to the annuitants for each product and the flexibilities and options they are allowed are also detailed for both the accumulation/deferral phase and the decumulation/payout phase of the annuity.

Table 1.1. **Classification of annuity products**

Product Type	Annuity Type	Accumulation		Payout	
		Guarantee	Option	Guarantee	Option
Fixed Payment	Level/Escalating/ De-escalating	Guaranteed return	Possible surrender	Guaranteed income; longevity	Possible surrender
	Advanced Life Deferred Annuity	Guaranteed return	None	Guaranteed income; longevity; purchasing power	None
	Joint	Guaranteed return	Possible surrender	Guaranteed income; longevity	Possible surrender
	Enhanced	X	X	Guaranteed income; longevity	None
Indexed Payment	Inflation	Purchasing Power	None	Purchasing power; longevity	None
	Participating	Minimum return	Possible surrender	Minimum income; longevity	Purchase additional guarantee with bonus
	Variable Payout	None	None	Longevity	None
Retirement savings with guaranteed income option	Variable Annuity	Minimum return	Surrender, withdraw, switch investment	Minimum income; longevity	Annuitisation, withdrawals, surrender
	Fixed Indexed Annuity	Minimum return	Surrender, withdrawals	Minimum income; longevity	Annuitisation, withdrawals, surrender

The first category of annuity products includes annuities promising fixed payments to the annuitant which are clearly defined from the onset of the contract and for which the underlying return does not change over time. These types of annuities typically offer full longevity protection to the individual as well as an implicit guaranteed return on the premium paid. However the annuitant generally has no flexibility with respect to the payments made or how the underlying assets are invested and no additional benefit is received if investment returns are higher than expected. The main risk for the annuity provider for these types of products guaranteeing payments for life is longevity risk. With respect to investment risk, the largest risk is reinvestment risk to the extent that the duration of the liabilities exceeds that of the assets.

The second category of annuity products includes those with indexed payments which vary depending on an external measure. These products allow annuity payments to increase or decrease depending on factors such as inflation or profits. This also means that the underlying return can vary over time, though a minimum rate is usually guaranteed. Annuitants can be exposed to volatility and unpredictability in their annuity payments, but can also benefit from changes in market conditions while having a certain minimum level of security. For products in this category, the mechanism with which payments are indexed and the level of risk-sharing offered play major roles in the overall risk exposure and the way in which the risk is managed by the annuity provider.

The final category of annuities is somewhat of a hybrid category, and includes products whose primary function is arguably retirement savings but which also offer the option of electing to receive a guaranteed level of income during retirement. These types of products can therefore also offer longevity protection. The return on these products depends on market performance, though minimum guarantees are typically offered. Furthermore, they offer the highest level of flexibility to the annuitant, providing access to the underlying assets and participation in positive market returns, as well as potential flexibility in the level of annuity income that is received. Nevertheless, this flexibility results in an increased risk to the annuity provider in terms of unpredictability of consumer behaviour, which complicates the management of the underlying investment risks. Furthermore the dynamic nature of the guarantees involved necessitates a rather complex risk management strategy to mitigate the investment risk exposure for the annuity provider. These factors may increase the cost of such guarantees for the consumer.

This chapter has laid out the scope, definitions and terminology to be used as the basis for the discussion of annuity products and their guarantees in the following chapters. Chapter 2 will provide an overview of the different types of products included in the classification from Table 1.1 and the different markets in which they can be found.

Notes

1. This requirement was removed in March 2014.
2. The exception to this would be a pension provider offering a guaranteed annuity conversion rate, which could be viewed as a deferred annuity product with the option to convert the accumulated assets into a stream of guaranteed payments.

Chapter 2

Overview of the different types of annuity products

This chapter provides an overview of the types of annuity products as well as select details on the markets in which they are found.

Level/(de)escalating annuities

Level fixed payment annuities are the most basic type of annuity, with fixed payments being guaranteed beginning immediately or deferred to some point in the future. Payments can also be scheduled to increase (escalate) or decrease (de-escalate) over time by a defined amount.

Despite being the most traditional type of product, the relative market for these types of annuities varies greatly across jurisdictions. In the United States, these types of annuities represented 12% of sales in 2012. In the United Kingdom, level immediate annuities accounted for 67.5% of compulsory conventional annuity sales in 2014, with escalating payment annuities representing less than 3% of all sales (The Chartered Insurance Institute, 2015). In Australia, the purchase of annuities with superannuation assets remains rather unpopular, and only two companies were still offering lifetime annuities as of 2013. Assets backing fixed level immediate life annuities in Australia totalled 4.9 billion AUD in 2012, representing only 0.3% of GDP. Term annuities are more popular than life annuities, with sales around ten times higher than life annuities in 2013, the vast majority of which had terms not exceeding five years (Asher, et al., 2013).

Advanced life deferred annuities

Advanced life deferred annuities (ALDAs), also known as longevity insurance, are deferred annuities which tend to be bought around retirement age with payments deferred to begin at a more advanced age, usually over age 75. This product behaves as a traditional annuity in that the premium is non-refundable and payments are only made if the person survives to the age to which payments were deferred. The advantage of these products for the customer is that they provide longevity insurance at a significantly cheaper price compared to purchasing an immediate annuity providing the same level of income.

A modified version of this product is the Deferred Income Annuity (DIA), which allows for shorter deferral periods, is not necessarily funded with a single premium, and offers additional options regarding death benefits and liquidity. The age at which annuity payments begin is typically defined at purchase.

DIAs represent a very small portion of the annuity market in the United States, with annual sales making up less than 1% of total annuity sales, though sales have been increasing rapidly since the product was introduced to the market (IRI, 2013). Recent regulation excludes the funds used to purchase a DIA from the minimum withdrawal calculation in IRAs, allowing for a lower annual withdrawal from the fund. This change may encourage the growth of this market in the United States.

While these types of products are in theory available as a payment option under Chile's individual retirement account system and are meant to be combined with programmed withdrawals up to the age at which the annuity payments begin, in practice the deferral period tends to be quite short.[1] Around a third of annuity premiums, or over 600 billion CLP, were paid go towards the purchase of these types of products in 2012.[2]

These types of annuities are not available in the UK, which some argue is a result of high risk-based solvency requirements and the lack of a financial instrument which can be used to hedge long-duration longevity risk (Blake and Turner, 2013). However, these arguments would also hold true for deferred annuities issued at younger ages.

Enhanced annuities

Enhanced annuities pay out a higher income level to individuals deemed to have a shorter life expectancy. Qualification for such an annuity can be based on the existence of a health impairment, such as high blood pressure or diabetes, or based on lifestyle factors such as tobacco use or socio-professional category. These products have the potential to increase the market for annuities by offering more attractive rates to individuals who would otherwise be likely to lose out from purchasing a regular immediate life annuity because their life expectancy is lower than the average of the annuitant population.

The largest market for enhanced annuities is in the United Kingdom, where the market has grown rapidly. These products represented nearly 30% of total annuity contracts sold in 2014 compared to only 7.7% in 2007 (The Chartered Insurance Institute, 2015). The increasing popularity has likely been due to the previous effective requirement to annuitise pension assets, as enhanced annuities would provide a solution for individuals for whom the requirement to purchase a regular annuity would represent a poor value given their longevity outlook. Offering these products could therefore provide an effective way to compete with standard annuities and gain market share.

The US market, where these types of annuities are known as substandard annuities, is much smaller. Less than 10% of annuity providers offer them, and as of 2005 they represented only 4% of the total immediate annuity contracts in force (LIMRA 2006). Furthermore, a large portion of these premiums seem to be used to provide premium financing arrangements rather than retirement income. These financing arrangements are essentially a way to arbitrage insurance premiums, which is not the intended purpose of these products and could potentially increase the anti-selection and concentration risk for the insurer. As a result some providers have pulled out of the US market.

Inflation indexed annuities

Inflation indexed annuities are annuities whose payments change depending on the rate of inflation each period. Compared to fixed level annuities, these annuities offer a much lower initial level income as payments will change in line with inflation each period.

In part as a result of lower initial payments, these types of annuities tend to be less popular than their level counterparts despite the added insurance of having a stable purchasing power. For example, less than 3% of all annuities sold in the United Kingdom in 2014 were indexed to inflation (The Chartered Insurance Institute, 2015). Some annuity providers in Australia are offering a partial indexation to inflation to try to improve the attractiveness of such protection, though the annuity market in Australia is quite small. Other jurisdictions, such as Chile and Mexico, require that life annuities be indexed to inflation and fixed level payment annuities are not an option.

Participating life annuities

Participating life annuities generally offer a minimum guaranteed level of income to the annuitant while offering additional bonus payments depending on an actual return or profit measure. These types of annuities therefore allow for some risk-sharing between the annuity provider and the annuitant, resulting in a lower cost to the insured but also higher uncertainty regarding the income which will be received.

One example of this type of annuity is the with profit annuities in the United Kingdom which vary the actual annuity payment depending on the performance of the underlying investment fund compared to a reference rate chosen by the policyholder. The assets backing the product are invested in the insurer's with-profit fund, so the policyholder is not in control of the investment decisions, and the insurer offers a guaranteed minimum level of income which typically assumes 0% return on investment. Furthermore, some of the gains in good years are retained by the insurer to be paid out in years of poorer performance, smoothing the annuitants' income from extreme volatility. These annuities proved quite popular leading up to the crisis, and generally outperformed traditional annuity offerings. However falling returns have reduced their popularity in more recent years as annuitants have seen their payments significantly reduced, and some providers have pulled out of the market. New premiums decreased by over 60% in 2014 compared to 2012 (The Chartered Insurance Institute, 2015).

Another variation of this type of annuity product is the participating payout life annuities (PLAs) in Germany, which offer a guaranteed minimum payment for life with the possibility of this amount increasing based on the insurer's realised profits. The minimum payment is calculated based on conservative assumptions which contain significant margins, so the existence of a surplus should be regularly expected. The profit participation of policyholders is not only based on investment gains but on all other profit sources. For example, payments may be increased by surplus coming from higher mortality experience than assumed. Individuals usually have the option of one of several formulas for profit participation. One option is to annuitize the surplus, in other words to increase the amount of the annuity and therefore also the minimum guaranteed payment. Another option is to receive the total surplus as a lump-sum payment, effectively topping up the guaranteed payment without impacting the future guarantee. Other combinations of these options also exist.

Deferred participating annuities often allow for regular contribution payments during the accumulation phase. The guarantee conditions of each of these contributions can also evolve over time with market conditions. This type of product design is common in the collective occupational schemes used in Denmark, for example.

Variations on annuities which offer similar profit-sharing features can be found in several other countries in Europe (e.g. Czech Republic, Estonia, Italy, Sweden) and profit sharing is at times imposed by regulation (e.g. Finland).

Variable payout annuities

Variable payout annuities, also known as variable immediate annuities and unit-linked annuities, are annuities for which the annuity payment varies along with asset returns. At purchase, the initial payment is calculated using a reference rate of return defined in the contract. Subsequent payments are adjusted by the ratio of the actual return on assets over the reference return, so if the market returns are higher (lower) than the reference return annuity payments will increase (decrease).

While this structure limits the investment risk for the insurer, the individual purchasing this type of annuity will be exposed to potentially high volatility of the annuity payments. However, this product does provide longevity insurance to the individual while offering the potential for benefit from high investment returns and indirect inflation protection, as well as potential control over the investment of the assets. Despite this, variable immediate annuities are less popular than their fixed counterparts.

A new variation on these types of products, the smoothed income annuity, has been more recently launched in Denmark and offers payments which vary depending on the underlying investment performance of individual accounts. These products aim to offer participation in market returns during both the accumulation and payout phase, while smoothing income using a clearly defined formula, thereby offering more transparency in the calculation of additional payments than a with-profits annuity does. This is accomplished by managing an individual buffer fund for each policy to absorb the impact of market volatility, and ultimately allows for a higher proportion of assets to be invested in equities, resulting in higher expected returns in the long run. At a minimum, the insurance company guarantees an annuity certain up to 25 years, but the insurance company may also offer additional return guarantees and/or longevity insurance with the product. Payments may also gradually be adjusted for future changes in mortality assumptions. This product represented 25% of pension sales for SEB Pension, which was the only company offering the product and has a market share in Denmark of around 10% (Pechter, 2013).

Variable annuities

Variable annuities, also referred to as segregated funds in Canada, are deferred retirement savings products with an annuity option. The underlying assets for these products are managed in individual accounts, usually with a variety of investment options, allowing for the realisation of market returns rather than locking in a fixed rate. A minimum rate at which the accumulated funds can be converted into an annuity is guaranteed at issue, though annuitisation is not mandatory and the policy may be surrendered instead. Optional guarantees are provided by the insurers which offer additional levels of protection from investment, mortality and/or longevity risk. These guarantees have become the distinguishing feature of variable annuity products.

Insurers typically hedge the investment risk of providing the guarantees for these products using financial derivatives. Following significant losses during the financial crisis, several providers who had not been sufficiently hedging their risk exited the market. Those that have remained have attempted to reduce the riskiness of the products by modifying their design, for example by limiting the number of investment options available, reducing the level of the guaranteed returns, and placing further restrictions on the amount and timing of withdrawals from the account.

The United States represents the largest market for variable annuities, and while sales decreased significantly during the crisis they subsequently rebounded to pre-crisis levels, reaching over USD 150 billion in 2011 (Geneva Association, 2013). Variable annuities represented 60% of all annuity sales in the second quarter of 2015. (IRI, 2015). Guaranteed lifetime withdrawal benefits (GLWBs) have been the most popular type of guarantee elected, attracting two-thirds of total guarantee sales in 2011 (Society of Actuaries and LIMRA, 2013).

Sales of segregated funds in Canada follow a sales pattern similar to that of the United States, though at a lower magnitude, with 2011 sales at around USD 11 billion (Geneva Association, 2013). The GLWB was introduced for segregated funds in Canada in 2007 and has proven to be extremely popular as an alternative to traditional annuitisation.

Similar types of the guarantees listed above have also been offered separately in the United Kingdom by insurance companies to provide investment and longevity protection for DC pension savings plans.

Variable annuities rapidly expanded in Japan in the early 2000's, with sales exceeding four trillion JPY in 2005. However following the financial crisis several high-profile insurers exited the market and sales have since declined dramatically, falling to less than 500 billion by 2011.

Variable annuities and their guarantees were introduced in Europe as well, but have not proven to be very popular and the growth of the market has been slow. Total technical provisions backing variable annuities amounted to less than €200 billion in early 2010.

Fixed indexed annuities

As annuity providers have sought to limit the risk of variable annuities but maintain the clear value proposition they offer to customers, fixed indexed annuities have gradually been growing in the market. These products offer returns which are indexed to the market along with downside protection through the same types of optional investment guarantees offered with variable annuities. The upside return is usually capped at around 4-5% for the customer.

For annuity providers these products generally offer lower risk than variable annuities as the investment fund selection is limited and the volatility is lower, resulting in more effective hedging of the downside investment risk.

Sales were USD 48 billion in the United States in 2014, an increase of nearly 24% from the previous year (Insured Research Institute, 2015). When offered with these products, the GLWB has proven continued popularity as an alternative to traditional annuitisation, being bought by 67% of customers purchasing fixed indexed annuities in 2011 where the option was available (Raham et al, 2012).

Table 2.1 shows the most common type of annuity product found in selected OECD countries.

Table 2.1. **Most common annuity product by jurisdiction**

Country	Most common product
Australia	Individual immediate fixed payment annuity with 10 year guaranteed period
Austria	Individual fixed payment deferred annuity
Belgium	Individual immediate annuity
Canada	Individual immediate fixed payment annuity
Chile	Individual inflation-indexed immediate annuity
Czech Republic	Individual indexed deferred annuity
Denmark	Group participating deferred annuity
Estonia	Individual participating deferred annuity
Finland	Individual participating deferred annuity
Greece	Individual fixed payment annuity
Hungary	Individual deferred fixed payment annuity
Israel	Individual annuity indexed to government bonds
Italy	Individual participating deferred annuity
Mexico	Individual inflation-indexed immediate annuity
Portugal	Individual fixed payment annuity
Spain	Individual fixed payment immediate annuity
Sweden	Participating deferred annuity
United Kingdom	Individual immediate fixed payment annuity
United States	Individual deferred variable annuity

Source: OECD Delegates to the WPPP/IPPC

Notes

1. "The OECD Roadmap for the Good Design of Defined Contribution Pension Plans" (OECD 2012) recommends combining programmed withdrawals with deferred life annuities as a solution for the payout phase.
2. Figures provided by the Superintendencia de Valores y Seguros (SVS).

References

Asher, A. et al. (2013), *Post retirement funding in Australia: B*. Sydney: Institute of Actuaries of Australia.

Blake, D., J. Turner (2013), "Longevity Insurance Annuities: Lessons from the United Kingdom", *Discussion Paper PI-1305 ISSN 1367-580X*, Pensions Institute, London.

The Chartered Insurance Institute, (2015), *Annuities insurance in the UK: Key trends and opportunities 2016*. Retrieved from *www.cii.co.uk/knowledge/resources/articles/annuities-insurance-in-the-uk,-key-trends-and-opportunities-to-2019/36857*

The Geneva Association (2013), "Variable Annuities – An Analysis of Financial Stability", The Geneva Association, Geneva.

Insured Research Institute (2015), "IRI Issues Fourth-Quarter and Year-End 2014 Annuity Sales Report".

Insured Retirement Institute (2013), "Deferred Income Annuities: Insuring against longevity risk", IRI.

LIMRA International, Ernst & Young (2006), "Substandard Annuities", LIMRA International and the Society of Actuaries, USA.

OECD (2012) "The OECD Roadmap for the Good Design of Defined Contribution Pension Plans", *www.oecd.org/finance/private-pensions/50582753.pdf*.

Pechter, K. (2013), "Have Your Danish, and Eat It Too", *Retirement Income Journal Vol. 221*, RIJ Publishing LLC, Emmaus, Pennsylvania.

Raham, C., et al. (2012), "The Annuity Landscape: Five trends to watch for in 2012 and 2013", Ernst & Young, USA.

Society of Actuaries, LIMRA (2013), "Variable Annuity Guaranteed Living Benefits Utilization: 2011 Experience", Society of Actuaries and LL Global, Inc., USA.

Chapter 3

The risks presented by annuity products and how they are managed

The chapter first provides a brief overview of the general approach to modern risk management. It then summarises the different types of risks which annuity providers can face. Finally, the risks specific to each type of annuity product are discussed in detail. This discussion addresses two aspects of the drivers of risk exposure and their management: the risks arising from the annuity product design and the assumptions used, and how the risk exposures can be controlled and mitigated going forward.

The different types of annuity products and the guarantees and options they offer to consumers present numerous risks which must be understood and managed by the annuity provider as well as understood by policy makers to ensure that appropriate regulation is in place. This chapter provides more in-depth descriptions of the types of products which were presented in the previous chapter, and goes into detail regarding how the risks presented by these products can be managed and mitigated.

Modern approaches to risk management

Modern risk management involves an active and conscious management of the various risks to which an annuity provider is exposed. This requires the provider to establish a clear risk policy detailing the risk management processes and procedures as well as the risk appetite of the provider, or in other words how much risk exposure they are willing and able to take on. The implementation of an effective risk policy requires that proper governance procedures are in place and that risk exposures are measured and quantified.

The governance of the risk management processes involves three lines of defence. The first is the management of the organisation and the assignment of accountability for the risk the provider takes. The second involves the various functions which inform the decisions taken by management, namely the risk management, actuarial and compliance functions. The third is the internal audit process, which independently evaluates compliance with the organisation's risk policy.

The quantification of risk is necessary to ensure that sufficient capital is being held to cover the risk exposures, and that these exposures do not exceed the risk appetite of the provider. A common approach to measure risk is the Value at Risk (VaR) approach, which quantifies the maximum loss of a given risk exposure at a certain confidence interval, for example an event expected every 1 in 200 years (99.5% VaR). In practice, annuity providers benefit from the diversification of risk across their various exposures, so these exposures will be aggregated taking this diversification benefit into account. For example, annuity providers can benefit from diversification of mortality and longevity risks, as these two risks can partially offset one another.

Nevertheless, the quantification of risk has its limitations, so purely quantitative approaches are usually complemented with a thorough internal analysis of all risks. This process is commonly called the Own Risk and Solvency Assessment (ORSA), and takes a more holistic view of the risk exposure of the annuity provider, also taking into account risks that are difficult or impossible to quantify.[1]

Risks faced by annuity providers

The main risks faced by annuity providers are longevity and investment related risks. Inflation also represents an important risk for products whose payments are indexed to the cost of living. Products offering increased flexibility for the customer can present increased risk with respect to consumer behaviour. Other risks such as underwriting risk, expense risk, operational risk or legal risk are more common across all product lines, though the drivers of these risks for annuity products may differ.

Longevity risk is traditionally one of the most significant risks for annuity providers, as annuity payments are promised for the lifetime of the individual. Longevity risk is a very long-term risk driven by the uncertainty around estimations of the future improvements in mortality. The annuity provider is exposed to risk of underestimating the improvements in mortality and the resulting increases in life expectancy, resulting in the need to make payments longer than provisioned for.[2]

Investment risks can also be significant for the annuity provider. Interest rate risk in particular can be significant for fixed payment annuity products, and is driven primarily by the potential mismatch between the duration of the assets held to back the annuity payments and the duration of the liabilities. The duration of the liabilities is generally longer, exposing the annuity provider to reinvestment risk that interest rates will have fallen when the assets, such as long-term bonds, arrive at maturity. Active asset-liability management (ALM) is necessary to manage this risk and to minimize the duration gap between assets and liabilities. Stress testing can be a useful tool in assessing the potential impact of changes in interest rates.

Interest rate risk compounds the effect of longevity risk on annuities, and the impact of low interest rates and longevity risk is larger than the sum of both, as low interest rates give a larger weight to the future and longevity risk increases with the time horizon considered. Therefore, the current economic environment of low interest rates can increase the risk exposure to the providers of annuity products.

Other investment risks to which the annuity provider can be exposed to relate to the risk of a fall in equity markets leading to a return on underlying assets below that of the return which is implicitly or explicitly guaranteed by the annuity product. These types of risks can be hedged through the use of financial derivatives. Credit risk exposure can also be present, with the annuity provider being exposed to the risk of default for corporate bonds or the default of a counterparty. Concentrations of exposures must therefore be carefully monitored.

Inflation risk for annuities indexed to inflation is evident as it increases the uncertainty around the level of future payments, and as with interest rate risk, is compounded by the existence of longevity risk. Inflation risk can be managed, however, through the purchase of inflation-linked bonds, though these instruments are not available in every jurisdiction. The limited availability or lack of inflation-linked bonds could pose a challenge to annuity providers offering inflation-indexed annuities.

Behavioural risk arises when the annuity product offers options to the customer, for example whether or not to withdraw from or surrender the product, whether to annuitise their accumulated assets or which underlying fund to invest in. Options come with risks due to the unpredictability of customer decisions relating to the timing and exercise of the options. These options can be quite costly to the insurer if the customer elects an option when the guarantee is 'in the money', that is when the value of the guarantee exceeds that of the invested assets in the account (for example when the insurer has guaranteed a 5% return on assets when the realised return was only 3%). When a policyholder has the option to surrender the annuity, the uncertainty that the actual surrender rates may differ from those assumed can also represent a large behavioural risk. While customer behaviour can be related to the value of the guarantees, setting accurate assumptions is difficult. Managing the risk from customer behaviour is usually best done at the product level with specific design features. For example, limiting the time at which customers can elect their options can reduce some uncertainty, and surrender charges reduce the probability that a customer will surrender their policy. However given the unpredictable nature of customer behaviour, it remains one of the most difficult risks for insurers to manage.

Underwriting risk is the risk of mispricing the product due to inappropriate assumptions, and potentially poses more of a challenge to certain types of annuities than for others. Enhanced annuities, for example, offer more attractive rates to individuals who would otherwise be likely to lose out from purchasing a regular, immediate life annuity because their life expectancy is lower than the average of the population. However, the insurer also takes a larger risk in terms of accurately pricing the annuity, as this is subject to an accurate assessment of the reduction in life expectancy for an individual given the specific qualifying condition.

Operational risk exposure is common across all product lines, and arises from a failure of internal processes or controls. However complex risk management strategies used for some types of annuity products, such as those relying on regular derivative trading, require a high level of expertise and sophistication to implement and therefore the annuity provider has to enforce strict governance and controls to mitigate the operational risk.

Legal risk may also be a consideration for annuity providers, along with the related reputational risk which could come with any legal action being made against the insurer. Several providers in the United Kingdom, for example, have faced claims of mis-selling annuity products which were inappropriate for the customers or for misrepresenting a product. These risks should be managed through clear guidelines for sales agents, careful consideration of the commission structures, and clear and transparent communication with customers.

Drivers of the risk exposures of annuity products

The drivers of the risk exposure of annuity products can be broken down into two aspects. The first is product design and the assumptions used to price the product, which determine the initial risks to which the annuity provider becomes exposed. This aspect is can be managed through product design features and rigorous assumption setting. The second driver of risk exposure is the potential for future experience to deviate from the assumptions used, which could result in insufficient assets to meet future payment obligations. Managing these risk exposures involves strategies to optimise and mitigate the risk. Table 3.1 presents the main risk drivers relating to each of these aspects for each type of product discussed in the previous chapter. The main tools which annuity providers can use to manage these risks are also included.

The remainder of this chapter will examine the risk management for each type of annuity product relating to these two aspects. Level life annuities, being the simplest type of annuity product, will be used as an example to demonstrate how the most basic risks in annuity products are managed. The examination of each subsequent product will explain how any changes in product design from this initial simple design may impact the risk exposure of the annuity provider, and where the risk management strategy may adapt as a result.

Table 3.1. **Risk drivers and risk management tools for annuity providers by product type**

Nature of Annuity	Annuity Type	Main Risk Drivers		Risk management tools
		Product design	Future exposure	
Fixed Payment	Level/Escalating/ De-escalating		Interest rates; longevity	Long term bonds; interest rate swaps; pooling; product diversification; surrender charges
	Advanced Life Deferred Annuity	Advanced age mortality assumptions	Interest rates; longevity	Long term bonds; interest rate swaps; pooling; monitoring longevity experience
	Joint	Joint longevity assumptions	Interest rates; joint longevity	Long term bonds; interest rate swaps; pooling; product diversification
	Enhanced	Impaired longevity assumptions	Interest rates; longevity; medical advances	Long term bonds; interest rate swaps; pooling; product diversification; monitoring longevity experience
Indexed Payment	Inflation	Caps	Inflation; longevity	Inflation linked bonds
	Participating	Surplus payment mechanism	Market returns; longevity	Conservative assumptions to set guarantee; investment strategy; smoothing; target bonus; participation rate
	Variable Payout	Mortality charge; AIR	Investment returns; longevity	Pooling
Retirement savings with guaranteed income option	Variable Annuity	See Table 3.2	Equity movements; interest rates; market volatility; longevity; customer behaviour	See Table 3.2; derivatives
	Fixed Indexed Annuity	Credited index rate formula	Equity movements; interest rates; longevity	Surrender penalty; capped return; long term bonds, derivatives

Risk management of annuity products

Risk management of fixed payment annuities

Fixed payment annuities represent the most basic type of annuity, offering a series of pre-defined payments for the lifetime of an individual in exchange for a premium. This type of annuity product offers little flexibility to the annuitant, who is generally limited in their ability to surrender the annuity following its purchase and otherwise has no access to the underlying assets or control over the investment strategy. The payment obligations of the annuity provider cease upon the death of the annuitant unless a minimum number of payments has been defined in the contract, in which case payments will be made until the later of the two events (death or the minimum duration of payments).

Level or (de)escalating life annuities are the most basic product and pay a fixed amount defined in advance for the lifetime of the individual. The other annuities within this category are simply slight variations of this basic model with respect to the risk profile of the annuitant(s). Advanced life deferred annuities are meant to defer payments to an advanced age, joint annuities depend on the survival of two lives and enhanced annuities offer a higher payment to individuals having a lower life expectancy due to health factors such as diabetes or lifestyle factors such as smoking.

Investment risk and longevity risk are the main risks which virtually all annuity products present to annuity providers, and the main risks which this category of products exhibits. The annuity provider wholly bears the investment risks as the payments to the annuitant are guaranteed in full, thereby implying an implicit guaranteed return. As payments are guaranteed for the lifetime of the individual, longevity risk is also fully borne by the annuity provider. Investment risk for fixed payment annuities is driven by the level of the implicit guaranteed return provided by the product, or in other words the discount rate which the annuity provider assumes in the pricing of the product. Longevity risk is driven by the extent to which annuitants live longer than the annuity provider assumes in the mortality tables it uses.

The risks and risk management for each of these products will now be discussed in turn. The ongoing risk management strategies for investment and longevity risk exposure are similar for all fixed payment annuity products. Therefore, these will be discussed primarily in the context of level or (de)escalating life annuities. Additional strategies will be discussed for individual products where these differ from level or (de)escalating annuities.

Risk management of level or (de)escalating life annuity

Risks from the product design and assumptions of a level or (de)escalating life annuity

The simplest fixed life annuity pays a stream of regular payments to an individual for his lifetime in exchange for a premium. These payments can be level, increasing or decreasing, so long as the amount of payments is defined in advance. Furthermore, payments could begin immediately, or be deferred to begin at some future point in time.

Generally speaking, the risk exposure for the annuity provider is driven by the assumptions used to price the product. The price of this product should be the net present value of expected future cash flows. For a promised regular payment of one unit of currency, the inputs for this exercise are therefore the discount rate, the expected survival of the individual and any expenses incurred by the annuity provider for offering the product. If experience does not align with these expectations, the price may not be sufficient to cover the future payments owed and the annuity provider will make a loss.

The exposure to investment risk is driven by the discount rate assumed for the annuity product. A discount rate is assumed in order to account for the time value of money, and implicitly represents the guaranteed return that the annuity provider is offering. Often the rate assumed is the risk-free rate. From a financial market perspective, this makes sense as products with the same expected cash flows should be sold at the same price, and the financial market asset which would replicate the guaranteed cash flows from an annuity would be a government bond paying regular coupons and returning the risk-free rate. Likewise, the annuity provider could invest the premium received in government bonds, and be sure that the bond payments would match the payments owed to the annuitant, which would be a risk-free investment strategy for the term of the bond(s).[3]

If the discount rate used to price the annuity is higher than the risk-free rate, the annuity provider is obliged to invest in higher risk assets offering a higher return in order to be able to meet the future payments. The annuity provider is therefore exposed to the risk that its investment returns fall below this guaranteed rate, and if this is the case the accumulated assets may not be sufficient to meet the guaranteed payments and the annuitant is exposed to credit risk. However the annuity provider could offer a lower price to the consumer by assuming a higher discount rate, which could potentially increase sales and market share. The difference between the actual investment return made from the invested premium and the discount rate assumed in the price of the annuity will represent a profit for the annuity provider, all else equal.

Investment risk is greater for annuities with a longer expected duration, for example those sold to individuals at a younger age, as the duration of liabilities is more likely to exceed the duration of the invested assets backing the products. This increased risk is mainly due to the reinvestment risk coming from a fall in interest rates, where assets must be reinvested in fixed-income instruments offering lower returns than those prevailing when the guarantees were promised.

Longevity risk exposure is driven by the mortality assumptions assumed by the annuity provider. For life annuities the expected survival of the individual must also be accounted for, since the annuity payments will be made for life. Thus when calculating the present value of expected future cash flows, the probability that the individual will survive to receive each cash flow has to be taken into account. These mortality assumptions generally vary by gender (unless regulation expressly forbids pricing by gender) and attained age. Improvements in mortality should also be assumed to account for the fact that mortality is expected to decrease over time (i.e. life expectancy is expected to increase).

Two main risks must be addressed in setting mortality assumptions: anti-selection and heterogeneity of the annuitant population. Voluntary annuity markets in particular are often exposed to the risk of anti-selection by consumers, in other words the tendency for individuals in better health who can expect to live longer lives to also be the ones most likely to purchase an annuity. Therefore the average survival for these individuals will be higher than that of the average of the population. If the annuity provider prices the annuity assuming the survival rate of the average population, it runs the risk of not having sufficient funds to pay future annuity payments which will have to be paid out longer than planned for. Some annuity providers may use 'select and ultimate' mortality tables, which assume lower mortality rates during the first years of the contract and gradually converge to average mortality rates, as the selection effect is not considered to be permanent.

Anti-selection risk could also potentially emerge where mortality assumptions used for pricing are not allowed to vary by gender. Females are known to have a higher life expectancy and therefore would expect to benefit more from an annuity paying a given level of income compared to a male having the same annuity. Males may therefore choose not to buy an annuity, eventually increasing the expected survival of the annuitants to the level expected for females. Anti-selection risk, however, is generally lower in mandatory annuity markets, since those purchasing an annuity would be more representative of the entire population on average.

Another risk in setting mortality assumptions is the heterogeneity of the annuitant population, particularly in terms of socio-economic characteristics. Individuals in higher socio-economic categories who are more likely to purchase larger annuities also tend to have higher life expectancies. This means that individuals having higher annuity payments will tend to live longer than those with lower annuity payments, and in the long run the annuity provider will have to pay higher annuity payments on average than it had planned for. In order to mitigate this risk, annuity providers often base mortality assumptions on annuity amounts paid rather than on the number of annuitants. In other words survival rates are calculated as the proportion of the total amount of annuity payments which are still expected to be paid at a future point in time, rather than as the number of people still expected to be alive. Since annuitants having higher annuity values generally live longer, this should result in higher survival estimates than would assumptions based on the number of people.

While surrender options are typically limited for these types of products, some products allow the annuitant to surrender the annuity during the deferral period and sometimes even during the payout phase. To mitigate the risk that the annuitants surrender the policy, annuity providers generally impose surrender penalties so that the annuitant is not entitled to the full value of the contract. These penalties can also vary depending on the prevailing interest rates, which affect the risk exposure of the annuity provider. In the United States, in particular, the Standard Non-forfeiture Law for Deferred Annuities requires and defines a minimum guaranteed value that must be provided by the annuity contract through the cash surrender value, partial withdrawals, or as a guaranteed minimum paid-up value for the future retirement date.

Annuity providers may also be exposed to expense risk, though this is not specific to annuity products. The annuity provider must make sure that the price of the product will cover the costs that it incurs to provide it. This includes overhead expenses, such as the salaries of the staff, as well as costs linked to the administration of the annuity policy itself. The present value of these expenses is deducted from the present value of future expected annuity payments to calculate the net present value of future cash flows. Accurate expense assumptions are difficult to achieve, however. For example, the estimation of how much overhead expense to allocate to the price of each annuity must take into account how many annuities are expected to be sold, and therefore if sales are not in line with expectations, annuity premiums may also not fully cover the annuity provider's expenses as planned. To mitigate this risk, annuity providers may allow for future variation in the expense fee charged to the annuitant, or even offer to buy back the annuity from the annuitant at an attractive rate.

Generally annuity providers may also include additional margins on assumptions to provide a cushion for adverse deviation in case the assumptions used for pricing are not exactly correct, making the expected average profit for the product positive and reducing the probability that the premiums received will not be sufficient to cover future annuity payments. This margin can also be gained from any additional investment return over the discount rate used for pricing.

Management of risk exposures for a level or (de)escalating life annuity

Once the annuity has been sold for the determined premium, the annuity provider must then manage the resulting risk exposures to maintain them at a level in line with its risk capacity. These risk exposures are primarily driven by the options and guarantees provided by the annuity product. For a fixed life annuity, these implicit guarantees are a fixed return on the premium paid – as defined by the discount rate used for pricing – and a guarantee against longevity risk where payments are made for the lifetime of the individual.

The investment strategy of the annuity provider is a core aspect of the risk management of annuity products. The investment strategy will drive the exposure to market and interest rate risks, and the investment strategy must be appropriate for the annuities which they are backing in terms of expected cash flows and the duration of the investment. The lowest risk strategy would be to simply invest in government bonds whose payments replicate the annuity payments. This strategy would allow the annuity provider to largely eliminate its risk exposure to interest rate movements and ensure that the implicitly guaranteed return will be met for the duration of the bond. However the annuity provider remains exposed to the risk of decreasing interest rates to the extent that it may be obliged to reinvest assets at a lower interest rate in the future to meet the annuity payments beyond the duration of the bond.[4] This reinvestment risk is higher in jurisdictions where very long term bonds are not available, as the annuity provider is not able to purchase assets which will match the expected duration of the annuity liabilities. Reinvestment risk is also larger for deferred annuities, which have a much longer duration than annuities which begin payments immediately, as well as for deferred annuities where premiums are received in regular payments during the accumulation phase rather than as a single upfront payment, as each of these premiums will have to be invested at the prevailing rate.

This situation in which the duration of the assets is less than the duration of liabilities is referred to as a negative duration gap and implies that the annuity provider is exposed to a fall in interest rates. In order to hedge against this risk, the annuity provider could enter into an interest rate swap agreement, where it agrees to pay a counterparty a future payment based on the prevailing interest rate at a future point in time (floating rate) in exchange for a payment based on the current interest rate (fixed rate). Under this contract, if the interest rate falls, the counterparty will pay the annuity provider the difference between the current interest rate and the lower future interest rate, ensuring that the annuity provider will still be able to meet the promised annuity rate and provide the implied return guarantee.

To illustrate how an interest rate swap works, consider an annuity provider who enters into a 10 year swap with a notional value of 1000 and the fixed payment based on current interest rates of 4%. The annuity provider agrees to make the floating payment to the counterparty in 10 years based on the future interest rate at that time, and the counterparty will pay the annuity provider the fixed payment of 4%*1000 = 40 at year 10. If the interest rate at year 10 falls to 3%, the net payment to the annuity provider will be (4% – 3%)*1000 = 10. If the interest rate at year 10 rises to 5%, the net payment to the annuity provider will be (4% – 5%)*1000 = –10, and the annuity provider will then make the net payment to the counterparty. The annuity provider therefore gives up the gain it would have otherwise received under a scenario of increasing interest rates in exchange for protection from the risk of decreasing interest rates.

While interest rate swaps can be effective at mitigating interest rate risk for the annuity provider, they also expose the annuity provider to the credit risk of the potential default of the counterparty. As such, swap rates tend to be slightly higher than government bond rates, as these rates include a risk premium as compensation for taking on credit risk. This credit risk exposure can be mitigated by requiring that collateral be put up to cover the expected payments of the swap. Meeting this collateral requirement, however, requires that the annuity provider maintain a sufficient level of liquidity in order to meet the margin calls. Interest rates swaps, however, generally make up only a part of the overall investment portfolio management for the annuity provider.

Many interest rate swap transactions are over-the-counter (OTC) transactions, though swaps are increasingly available on exchanges. Using exchange traded derivatives could increase the transparency and liquidity of such transactions by providing a level of standardisation and a centralised platform on which to perform transactions. Clearing the transactions through central counterparties can also reduce the credit risk exposure from these instruments. Recent regulations such as the Dodd-Frank Act in the United States and the European Market Infrastructure Regulation (EMIR) in Europe are driving increased transparency and collateralisation requirements to mitigate this risk.

The annuity provider is also exposed to longevity risk from an annuity, and if experienced mortality turns out to be lower than assumed for pricing and reserving, the annuity provider will have to make annuity payments longer than planned for. Annuity providers may require medical disclosure for annuitants to better assess their life expectancies, particularly those with high contract values. Assuming that the underlying mortality assumptions are accurate, the annuity provider can expect that the actual annuity payments made will be in line with expectations on average. The main risks to manage going forward are therefore the risks of the volatility of mortality experience and the risks that the trend in mortality (mortality improvement) deviates from expectations.

Volatility risk could result in actual payments diverging from expectations simply due to the underlying volatility of mortality experience. This risk reduces as the number of annuitants increases and the longevity risk is pooled across a larger group of individuals.

Longevity risk exposure is also driven by differences in the assumed and realised trend of mortality improvement over time. If realised mortality improvements are higher than expected, the annuity provider will have underestimated life expectancy and will have to make payments for longer than planned for. This risk is relatively larger for annuity contracts with a longer expected duration, for example deferred annuities, as there is much more uncertainty around what the mortality will be in 30 years' time than in 10 years.

The annuity provider can partially mitigate longevity trend risk by diversifying its business with products having payments contingent on mortality, for example life insurance products which pay a sum to beneficiaries upon the death of the insured individual. This is because if mortality improvements are higher than expected, annuitants are living longer but on the other hand individuals purchasing life insurance are also dying less. Nevertheless this remains an imperfect hedge as the two types of products tend to target different age groups; life insurance tends to cover middle aged adults and annuities tend to be paid out to retired people. Historical analysis shows that mortality improvements can differ quite significantly across age groups and cohorts, and in many countries ages 60-75 have recently been experiencing the highest level mortality improvements, resulting in a potentially larger exposure to longevity risk for annuity business than the mortality contingent business could offset.

The annuity provider can also choose to transfer its longevity risk to a third party.[5] As with all risks traditionally insured by a life insurer, longevity risk can be passed on to a reinsurer, who would commit to paying future annuity payments owed in exchange for a premium for accepting this risk. Alternative solutions to transfer longevity risk to a third party are beginning to emerge in practice, however, particularly in the United Kingdom and in the Netherlands. Annuity providers can enter into longevity swap contracts, where actual annuity payments based on realised mortality improvements are paid by the counterparty in exchange for fixed payments from the annuity provider based on expected mortality assumptions established at the beginning of the contract. If mortality improves at a higher rate than expected, the counterparty would then pay the additional annuity payments implied by the longer survival rates. However, if mortality improvements are lower than expected, the annuity provider would owe the difference in expected and actual payments to the counterparty, forfeiting the gain they would have had otherwise due to their overestimation of life expectancy.

Longevity swaps can be bespoke, based on the actual realised mortality of the annuitant population, or index-based, where the payments made by the counterparty to the annuity provider are based on an independent and objective longevity index, normally based on the mortality of the general population. Bespoke transactions completely transfer the longevity risk from the annuity provider to the third party, as the payments made by the counterparty should exactly match the annuity payments owed given the realised mortality of the underlying annuitant population. Annuity providers retain some of the longevity risk if an index-based longevity swap is employed, however, as the mortality improvements of the index will not necessarily follow the mortality improvements actually experienced by the annuitant population. If the annuitant population experiences higher improvement than the general population on which the index is based, the annuity provider will still have to make additional annuity payments on top of the payment received from the counterparty to meet its annuity payment obligations. This residual longevity risk retained from an index-based longevity swap is referred to as longevity basis risk.

With both bespoke and index-based longevity swaps, however, the annuity provider gains exposure to credit risk since there is a risk that the counterparty could default on its payments. As with interest rate swaps, this risk can be mitigated with well-designed collateral requirements which would have to be set aside to be accessible to the annuity provider as needed to meet expected payments.

Risk management of advanced life deferred annuities

Risks from the product design and assumptions of advanced life deferred annuities

Advanced life deferred annuities (ALDAs) are meant to be purchased at or near retirement, with payments deferred at least 10 to 15 years to begin at an advanced age, usually after age 75. While in design it is the same in principle to a regular fixed deferred annuity, the advanced life deferred annuity can be viewed more as a pure longevity insurance product, and it can be bought at a significant discount to a fixed immediate annuity beginning at retirement. This is because individuals who die before receiving payments heavily subsidise those who survive to receive payments, and many who survive will only receive payments for a small number of years. The ALDA's main purpose is to protect the individual from running out of finances in old age and not to provide a steady stream of income throughout retirement.

Given that the ALDA is meant to begin payments at an advanced age, its pricing is heavily dependent on mortality assumptions at advanced ages. However, mortality data is not widely available for ages over 85 and mortality rates at advanced ages rely heavily on estimations based on extrapolation models. There is no clear consensus by demographers as to the expected pattern of mortality at the oldest ages and numerous extrapolation models exist which result in wide variations in estimated mortality. The estimation of mortality at these advanced ages is therefore subject to significant model risk.

The longevity risk exposure faced by the annuity provider from ALDA products is therefore potentially large and difficult to accurately quantify. To illustrate the impact that the overestimation of mortality rates could have on the actuarially fair premium of an ALDA, consider a level annuity purchased at age 65. If mortality is overestimated by 5%, corresponding to an underestimation of life expectancy by approximately 5.4 months, the reserves needed to cover the annuity liability for an annuity beginning payments immediately will only increase by about 1%. If payments are deferred to age 80, reserves will need to increase by 3%, and if payments will begin at age 85 reserves will need to increase by over 4%.[6]

Management of risk exposures for advanced life deferred annuities

The primary difference in the management risk exposures for ALDAs and those of level deferred annuities stems from the age profile of the annuitants. Mortality experience should be carefully monitored to ensure that experience, particularly at the older ages, does not significantly differ from the mortality assumptions assumed. Where deviations are observed, assumptions would need to be updated for new sales.

Risk management of joint-life annuities

Risks from the product design and assumptions of joint-life annuities

Annuity payments from joint-life and survivor annuities are identical to level or (de) escalating annuities, except that the payments depend on the survival of two lives rather than one individual, with the second life typically being the spouse of the main annuitant. Payments can continue in full until the death of both individuals, or alternatively be reduced upon the first death.

The only difference in the risk profile of joint-life annuities from an individual life annuity is that two survival rates must be considered when determining the price of the product, and assumptions must be made regarding the gender and age of the second individual if these factors are not known in order to determine his or her expected survival rates. While the independence of mortality of each spouse is commonly assumed, much evidence points to the fact that the survival of spouses is not independent and married people in general tend to have lower mortality rates (Johnson et al, 2000). Three main types of dependencies are commonly identified (Ji et al.,2012; Spreeus and Owadally, 2013). The first is dependence of mortality linked to commonly experienced events, for example spouses have a higher chance of dying in the same car accident. The second is linked to a shared environment resulting in similar levels of exposure to longer-term risks, for example living in a house with asbestos or having shared lifestyle factors such as diet. The third dependency is a short-term dependence following the death of one of the spouses. Often called the 'broken-heart syndrome', evidence shows that following the first death the surviving spouse has a higher mortality risk, though this increased risk diminishes over time and is more pronounced for surviving males than for females.

This dependency of mortality between spouses implies that annuity contracts could be potentially mis-priced if relying on the assumption of the independence of mortality, but due to the complexity of establishing joint mortality assumptions it is not clear to what extent they are used in practice. Furthermore, the drivers of dependence could work in different directions and it is not clear that lower overall survival, which would imply an increased risk to the annuity provider, would result.

Management of risk exposures for joint-life annuities

Again the main difference in the management of risk exposures for joint-life annuities compared to level payment annuities for an individual life is the mortality profile of the annuitant(s). Therefore continuous monitoring of mortality experience should be performed to ensure that experience remains in line with the mortality assumptions being assumed.

Risk management of enhanced annuities

Risks from the product design and assumptions of enhanced annuities

Enhanced annuities offer a higher level of guaranteed income for individuals who can expect to have a shorter than average life expectancy due to certain health conditions such as diabetes or lifestyle factors such as smoking. Again, the only difference with level or (de) escalating fixed annuities is the mortality assumptions assumed in the product.

Two main risk management challenges arise with the offer of enhanced annuities. The first is setting accurate mortality assumptions based on specific health conditions or lifestyle factors, and the second is the potential increase in anti-selection for regular annuity products.

Establishing survival expectations for enhanced annuities can be challenging for several reasons. Firstly, mortality data which are linked to details regarding underlying health conditions or socioeconomic categories are not widely available. Secondly, even where data is available, estimations of mortality will be based on smaller population sets and may therefore be subject to a larger risk of misestimation than are rates based on a larger population. Finally, medical advances are constantly evolving and people may be able to live much longer with a given condition in the future than is possible today, meaning that assumptions based on experience may not prove to be accurate in the future. Establishing accurate mortality assumptions and continuous monitoring of experience therefore becomes key to managing the risks to which the annuity provider becomes exposed.

Management of risk exposures for enhanced annuities

Continuous monitoring of experience is necessary to be able to ensure that assumptions are accurate and up-to-date, not only for the enhanced annuities being offered but also for the pricing of regular annuities. The emergence of a market for enhanced annuities could also change the risk profile of the individuals purchasing regular annuities. Individuals having any health condition who would have normally purchased a regular annuity could instead purchase an enhanced annuity to have a larger income. As a result, the average life expectancy of individuals purchasing regular annuities could increase, and past experience may no longer be a reliable source of data on which to base mortality assumptions, exposing the annuity provider to additional pricing risk with respect to longevity.

Risks posed by indexed payment annuities and how they are managed

The payments for indexed payment annuities are not defined in advance; rather they vary depending on the movement of some external index. The level of annuity payments is therefore uncertain and will vary over time. These types of annuities provide some level of market exposure to the annuitant, and can bring in a risk-sharing mechanism where the annuity provider passes on some of the investment and/or longevity risk to the individual. However, the uncertainty in future payments can also result from an additional guarantee for the annuitant in the product, like inflation-linked annuities.

The types of indexed annuities discussed here will be those with payments linked to inflation (inflation-linked annuities), to the annuity provider's profits (participating annuities), or simply to the investment performance of the fund in which the underlying assets are invested (variable payout annuities).

Whether the uncertainty of payments increases the investment risk exposure of the annuity provider depends on whether the uncertainty stems from a risk which the annuity provider is insuring the annuitant against, as with inflation-linked annuities, or whether the uncertainty is a result of risk-sharing between the annuity provider and the annuitant, as with participating and variable payout annuities. For the former, the annuity provider bears the risk of having to make higher payments than expected in periods of high inflation; however with the latter the annuity provider is able to reduce payments if market returns or profits are lower than expected. The annuity provider's exposure to investment risk is therefore higher for inflation-linked annuities and lower for participating and variable payout annuities compared to fixed payment annuities.

The longevity risk exposure of the annuity provider also depends on whether a risk-sharing mechanism is incorporated in the product design. The longevity exposure for inflation-linked annuities remains the same as for fixed payment annuities. However systemic longevity risk can be shared with the annuities for participating and variable payout annuities, thereby reducing the overall longevity risk exposure for the annuity provider.

Risk management of inflation-linked annuities.

Risks from the product design and assumptions of inflation-linked annuities

Annuity payments can be linked to an inflation index, guaranteeing that the individual will be able to maintain the same purchasing power throughout retirement. The initial payment from an inflation-linked annuity will be much lower than for a level payment annuity, given the same purchase price, as payments could increase every year depending on inflation. Since payments are not known in advance and there is high uncertainty regarding the future levels of inflation, inflation-linked annuities will also typically be more expensive than an escalating annuity with payments increasing at a known fixed rate.

Guarantees offering protection from uncertain future financial market risks can be valued using stochastic models, which can capture the inherent uncertainty by valuing the guarantee across many possible future scenarios. The average present value of expected future cash flows of an inflation-indexed annuity across all stochastic scenarios will generally be higher than the value under a deterministic scenario, representing the additional cost of providing the guarantee given the future uncertainty.

Management of risk exposures for inflation-linked annuities

In terms of the investment strategy for inflation linked annuities, equities alone have been shown to be an imperfect hedge for inflation, and can even be negatively correlated with inflation over the short to medium term (Tiong, 2013). Annuity providers could hedge their exposure to inflation risk by investing in inflation-linked bonds in jurisdictions where such bonds are available. However investing in inflation-linked bonds alone will drag down investment returns in periods of low inflation, so a combination of these bonds and equities could represent a more efficient investment strategy for managing the risk exposure to inflation.

Risk management of participating annuities

Risks from the product design and assumptions of participating annuities

Annuity payments may also be linked to the profits realised by the annuity provider, allowing the annuitant to participate in any surplus resulting from additional gains over the assumptions used for pricing the product. The annuity payments therefore can be broken down into two parts: a guaranteed portion behaving as a regular level annuity plus a variable portion depending on the realised investment and/or mortality experience.

This design allows annuity providers to pass on some of the investment and longevity risk to the individual, as annuity providers can include more significant margins in their assumptions for the calculation of the guaranteed portion of annuity income with the expectation that a portion of those margins will be passed back to the individual unless they are needed to cover adverse deviations in experience. In this way, participation functions as a mechanism for sharing long-term systemic risks between the annuity provider and the individual, such as with respect to longevity risk. As annuitants will be sharing those potential risks, rules concerning consumer protection may need to be in place to ensure that the underlying mechanisms are clear and transparent.

The variable non-guaranteed portion of annuity income can be paid to the consumer in one of two ways: it can either be taken as a bonus payment in each period or be used to increase the guaranteed level of income. The former arrangement poses the least risk to the annuity provider, as it incurs no additional liability to the annuitant in the future, whereas an increase in the guaranteed income will also increase the future liabilities and therefore the exposure to investment and longevity risk. Any additional guaranteed future income resulting from the participation bonus can be based on the guarantees initially stated in the contract, or based on prevailing interest rates and longevity assumptions at the time the guarantee is increased. If based on the initial guarantees, the annuity provider is more exposed to the reinvestment risk from potential decreases in the interest rate, as the bonus payment will have to be reinvested at the lower prevailing rates while guaranteeing an income implying a higher return. If the increased guarantee is based on current assumptions, the level of risk-sharing defined at the beginning of the contract will be able to be maintained.

Deferred participating annuities may also benefit from profit participation during the accumulation phase, with similar implications with respect to the relative risk exposure depending on the way the participation is paid to the annuitant and the level of guarantees offered on the bonus payment. As with fixed annuities, however, the risk exposure is greater due to the longer duration of the contract and the increased uncertainty particularly with respect to longevity assumptions, especially where bonus payments are offered the same level of guarantees provided at the onset of the contract.

The duration of the guarantee could potentially be revised after a defined number of years to limit some of the reinvestment and longevity risk exposure for the annuity provider. For example, the initial guarantee could be for ten years, with a revision of the guaranteed terms at the ten year mark based on prevailing interest rate and longevity assumptions, with the new guarantee terms being applicable for another ten years.[7] To the extent that these types of annuity contracts are funded via regular contributions, i.e. each contribution was guaranteed for ten years at the prevailing rate, this would also help to automatically smooth any changes to the total guaranteed payment eventually made to the individual.

Management of risk exposures for participating annuities

The level of the guaranteed return for the participating annuities is the main driver of the underlying risk exposure to annuity providers. As with fixed payment annuities, the higher the guarantee the more likely the actual investment return will fall below the return guaranteed to the annuitant and therefore the more risk the annuity provider is exposed to. Countries tend to differ with respect to the level of guarantee typically provided. With profit annuities in the United Kingdom, for example, tend to guarantee only a 0% rate of return whereas Germany stipulates a maximum allowed guaranteed return for its participating life annuities based on recent interest rates.

The level of non-guaranteed payment will depend on the participation rate specified, which defines what percentage of profits is shared with the annuitants. Regulation may stipulate a minimum participation rate, as is the case in Germany.

Having a variable non-guaranteed portion of the annuity income for participating annuities implies that the individual is exposed to the potential volatility of his annuity payments. Two underlying mechanisms can contribute to the actual level of income volatility experienced by the annuitant. First of all, accounting rules which dictate the way in which the profits are defined for the calculation can result in more or less volatility of surplus. Secondly, the annuity provider may build up an additional reserve with surplus retained during high periods of profitability to be paid to the annuitant in periods of low profitability with the objective of providing a more stable income stream. Both of these mechanisms have implications for the risk exposure of the annuity provider.

Accounting rules impact the volatility of the balance sheet and the reported surplus on which the non-guaranteed portion of the annuity income will be based. They also influence the probability that the annuity provider's capital will fall below zero, referred to as the shortfall probability.

Accounting rules requiring assets to be valued at historical cost report only realised gains and losses for the surplus calculation and result in lower balance sheet volatility. Historical cost accounting therefore automatically results in less volatile non-guaranteed payments to the annuitant. However, relying on only the historical cost method is not optimal for the annuitant as profits from equity investment are not realised and passed on through the non-guaranteed annuity payments until the equity is sold.

Fair value accounting, on the other hand, requires assets to be valued at current prices and takes unrealised gains and losses into account for the calculation of the surplus, resulting in a higher volatility of the non-guaranteed annuity payment. This method also increases the shortfall probability of the annuity provider, as it would have to pay part of its unrealised profits to the annuitant in positive surplus years while bearing the unrealised losses when the surplus is negative (Maurer et al., 2014).

The annuity provider may establish a separate buffer reserve for the annuity payments as a way to reduce the volatility of the total annuity payments from any volatility in the surplus. The annuity provider could then build up the reserve in periods of higher profitability so as to be able to draw on this reserve in order to sustain total annuity payments at a targeted level even in periods of low profitability. By allowing for an extra buffer to meet not only bonus payments but the guaranteed payments in times of poor market returns, this type of smoothing technique can increase the profitability and decrease the probability of shortfall for the annuity provider. Nevertheless, while smoother annuity payments could be highly valued by a risk adverse individual, smoothing also potentially reduces the total expected benefits, as amounts withheld in periods of positive surplus may exceed those paid out during negative periods. Generally the underlying parameters relied upon to distribute surplus payments to annuitants and credit buffer reserves can vary widely from one annuity provider to the next, though minimum participation rates or limits on asset allocations may be imposed by regulation.

The risk that the annuity provider will not have sufficient assets to cover the guaranteed rate and will experience a shortfall is driven by several factors relating to the mechanism by which the reserves are managed and non-guaranteed payments defined. These factors include exposure to equity, the target level of the annuity payments where smoothing is imposed (the guaranteed plus variable amount) and the minimum profit participation rate. The extent to which the probability of shortfall is influenced by each of these factors is largely a function of the financial strength of the annuity provider.

The target payment and the exposure to equities can both be modified to change the risk exposure of the annuity provider. Kling et al. (2007) show that highly capitalised companies can easily maintain the probability of shortfall at a given level with minor adjustments to either the equity exposure or the target bonus payments, whereas poorly capitalised companies do not have much flexibility and must maintain lower levels of both variables to ensure sufficient reserves. Furthermore the shortfall probability is not sensitive to changes in the target bonus when reserve levels are low. However the shortfall probability is highly sensitive to the exposure to equities for less well capitalised companies, implying that the investment strategy should be dynamic based on reserve levels, with equity exposure being decreased as reserve levels fall.

The relationship between the guaranteed return and the target return is another dynamic to consider for the risk exposure of the annuity provider. Annuity contracts with higher guaranteed rates imply a higher risk exposure for the annuity provider than contracts with low guaranteed rates. From the annuitants' perspective, those with lower guarantees are exposed to a larger risk of a decrease in total annuity payments. To compensate for this and have comparable risk exposure for contracts with different guarantee levels, higher bonus payments could be targeted for annuitants having lower guarantees, offering these contracts higher payments during periods of high surplus to make up for lower payments in low-return environments. This result is again dependant on the financial strength of the company, as the increase in risk with the increase in guaranteed return is less pronounced in highly capitalised companies, implying that these companies have less of need to differentiate the surplus payments across contracts (Kling et al., 2007). Different target bonus calculations for different generations of contracts could also be imposed to prevent intergenerational risk transfer across annuity contracts – to older generation contracts with higher guarantees from more recent generations with lower guarantees – which could be perceived as unfair.

Following the argument of varying the target level of return across contracts with different levels of guarantees, one could also argue that contracts having higher guaranteed returns should have a lower rate of participation in the surplus.

The level of participation rate will also influence the annuity provider's risk exposure. Imposing a minimum level of participation reduces the flexibility the annuity provider has in its decision of how to distribute the surplus. Imposing a high minimum participation rate could have a negative impact on risk exposure to the extent that the annuity provider is not able to build up its buffer reserve. This could occur, for example, under a fair value accounting regime where the annuity provider would be obliged to distribute a larger portion of its assets each period to the annuitants (Kling et al., 2007). The annuity provider would then be more exposed to market shocks, and increase the likelihood that the annuitant would have his future annuity payments cut. Maurer et al. (2014) show that the annuitant's utility is relatively insensitive to the participation rate employed, so higher participation rates do not necessarily make the annuitant better off. A lower participation rate implying a lower risk to the annuity provider may then be preferable.

The calculation of the non-guaranteed annuity amount which is actually paid to the annuitants is often not completely clear or transparent, particularly where smoothing mechanisms are implemented, and can be decided with a level of subjectivity by the annuity provider. This lack of predictability and transparency of actual bonus payments received could present problems with respect to consumer protection and ensuring that the annuitant is fully aware of the risk that his total annuity payments could decrease, particularly for contracts offering a low guaranteed rate such as the with profit annuities in the United Kingdom. In an attempt to increase transparency, Denmark has issued guidelines on how to fairly distribute the surplus between shareholders and policyholders, but full transparency is difficult to achieve in practice given the numerous variables involved.

Risk management of variable payout annuities

Risks from the product design and assumptions of variable payout annuities

Variable payout annuities (VPAs) promise annuity payments which are indexed to the underlying fund in which the assets are invested. Annuity payments therefore increase and decrease with movements in the market, and the annuitant can benefit from investment gains over time. Nevertheless, annuitants can potentially experience high volatility in their annuity payments and are exposed to the risk that annuity payments will significantly decrease in a given period. The annuity payments, however, are guaranteed for life so the annuitant is protected from longevity risk.

The initial payment from a variable payout annuity is based on an assumed investment rate (AIR), which can be defined by the annuity provider or chosen by the annuitant. The higher the AIR is, the higher the initial payment will be. Each subsequent payment is adjusted relative to this target return, so if a high target return is chosen the future growth of the annuity payment will be limited compared to an annuity having a low target return. Furthermore annuity payments are more likely to decrease in the future given a high AIR.

As an example of how each subsequent payment is calculated, consider an AIR of 2% and an investment return on the underlying fund of 5%. The subsequent annuity payment will increase by 3%, which is the additional return realized over the assumed return. However if the AIR is 4%, the payment will only increase by 1%. While lower AIRs result in lower initial payments, payments after several years will be higher than for annuities with high AIRs as payments will be increasing at a higher rate.

Figure 3.1 illustrates the hypothetical payments of a variable payout annuity assuming AIRs of 2%, 4% and 6%. The figure clearly shows that while initial payments for annuities with low AIRs is smaller, payments also end up being significantly larger in the long run than for annuities with high AIRs. The choice of the AIR therefore must consider whether higher income is needed earlier in retirement or later.

Figure 3.1. **Illustrated evolution of annuity payments for a VPA beginning at age 65**

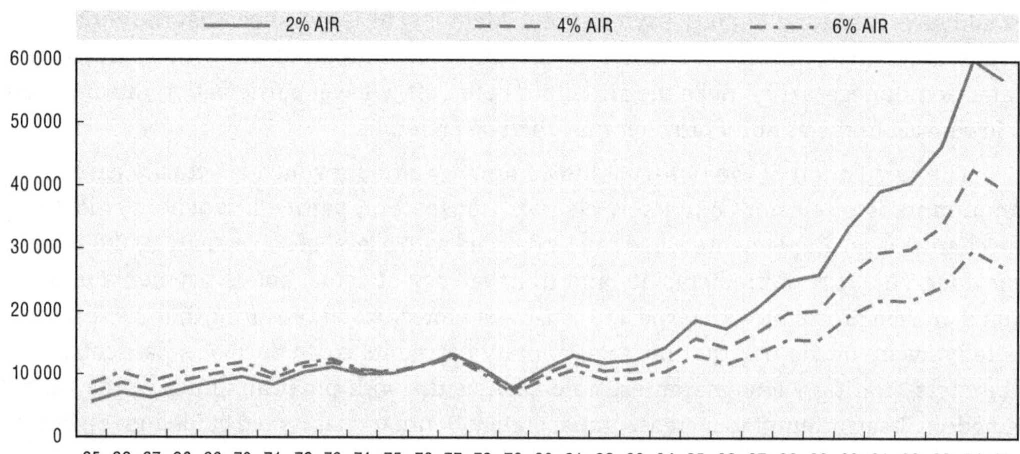

Source: Initial payments as calculated in Milevsky (2002) based on a 100 000 premium at age 65 and returns based on the S&P 500 index from 1960.

This illustration has ignored the longevity risk and expenses incurred by the annuity provider. In calculating the adjusted payment for each period, the annuity provider may also deduct a charge for assuming the longevity risk of the pool of annuitants as well as a charge to cover the administration fees. These charges may be defined at the onset of the contract – in which case the annuity provider fully assumes the longevity risk of the annuitants – or adjusted each period based on actual longevity experience and expenses incurred. If actual longevity experience is deducted, the systemic longevity risk is passed on to the annuitants, since increased payments due to mortality improvements which turn out to be higher than expected can be offset by reducing the adjustment to the annuity payment for the subsequent periods. Annuitants are still protected from idiosyncratic longevity risk however, that is the risk that they as individuals will live longer than average, as they will continue to receive annuity payments for their lifetimes.

Management of risk exposures for variable payout annuities

To the extent that charges deducted from the adjustments to annuity payments are updated to account for realised mortality, the annuity provider passes on the systemic longevity risk to the annuitants. This requires active monitoring and updating of the mortality charge. Assuming an annuitant pool of sufficient size, the provider's exposure to idiosyncratic longevity risk should also be quite limited, since the larger number of annuitants there are in the pool the less likely that the average lifespan of the annuitants will exceed the life expectancy assumed by the provider.

Investment risk is shared with the annuitants through the adjustments to the annuity payments. However, providing an initial payment based on a positive AIR means that some of the expected investment returns are being advanced to the annuitant and the subsequent adjustments will not immediately offset any decrease in investment performance. The annuity provider thus retains some of the investment risk for the product. The higher the AIR is, the longer it will take for the adjustments in payments to offset any lower than expected investment performance. The annuity provider therefore assumes more investment risk for annuities having higher AIRs. This risk should be accounted for by increasing the level of invested assets accordingly.

Risks posed by retirement savings products with a guaranteed income option and how they are managed

The class of retirement savings products considered here encompasses both the accumulation/saving phase and the drawdown phase of retirement financial planning. In contrast to traditional retirement savings or pension products, however, these types of products offer an option (rather than a requirement) to receive a guaranteed level of income in the future based on the level of assets accumulated and a conversion rate defined at the onset of the contract. Because of this feature, these products resemble a deferred annuity product and qualify as annuity products.

The main difference between these types of products and the deferred annuities classified as having fixed or indexed payments is that here the underlying assets are not completely relinquished to the annuity provider and the individual retains more flexible access to the capital. Thus the annuities in the category resemble long-term savings products. Furthermore, because converting the accumulated assets into a guaranteed income stream is optional, the accumulated assets may be withdrawn as a lump sum and the product may never provide annuity payments.

Two annuity products are discussed in this category: variable annuities and fixed indexed annuities. These products vary in terms of the level of guarantees and flexibility offered. The higher the level of guarantees or flexibility, the higher the risk exposure is for the annuity provider, and the more complex the risk management strategy becomes. The cost of these products therefore also increases as a result. Variable annuities tend to have higher levels of flexibility than fixed index annuities, necessitating a more involved risk management program. Both types of annuities will be covered in this section.

These types of products often offer a guaranteed return on investment during the accumulation phase for the purpose of converting assets into an income stream, exposing the annuity providers to investment risk as with the other categories of products. However, for these products the individual may have a say in how the assets are invested, so the annuity provider may not be able to fully control the investment strategy or the level of investment risk to which it is exposed. As a result these types of products require a more complex investment risk management strategy than the other product categories, and the risk is often managed through the use of hedging instruments such as derivatives.

The exposure that annuity providers have to longevity risk from these types of products depends on whether or not the annuity option is elected. If the annuitant never ends up electing to receive annuity payments at the end of the accumulation period, the annuity provider will not be exposed to longevity risk. However, as these types of products are deferred and tend to have longer expected durations, the longevity risk can be potentially quite large to the extent that the annuity option is elected.

The options and flexibility offered with these types of products expose the annuity providers to policyholder behaviour risk at a level which the other classifications of products are not exposed.[8] These risks include the rates at which policyholders choose to withdraw from their account or surrender their policy and the timing of these, how they choose to invest their assets, and the time at which they choose to begin receiving annuity payments (if at all). Policyholder behaviour which is not in line with assumptions may not only increase the cost to the annuity provider of meeting the guarantees, but may also reduce the effectiveness of the annuity provider's hedging strategy for its investment risks. Furthermore behaviour tends to be difficult to predict and the risk is not easily managed.

Risk management of variable annuities

Risks from the product design and assumptions of variable annuities

Variable annuities (or segregated funds as they are known in Canada) are essentially individual investment accounts for which the individual has the future option to convert accumulated assets into a lifetime annuity at a pre-determined guaranteed rate, and for which annuity provider can offer optional minimum income guarantees. The product therefore offers two distinct phases: an accumulation phase meant to grow the asset base, and the drawdown phase where income is taken from the product, unless a lump sum is taken from the product at the end of the accumulation phase. The individual maintains access to his assets during the accumulation phase and is allowed to withdraw funds, though the contract may specify limitations or penalties for doing so. For traditional variable annuity products, the invested assets are held by the insurer, though with the more recent contingent deferred annuities, the income guarantees are provided for an alternative investment vehicle held by the individuals themselves. These products offer a guaranteed rate at which the accumulated assets are converted into an income stream for the drawdown phase.

This guaranteed conversion rate varies by the age at which the assets are annuitised to maintain actuarial neutrality.

In addition to the basic guaranteed annuity conversion rate, optional guarantees are usually offered with the product that vary based on how the accumulated assets will be paid out. These can guarantee a minimum payment to the beneficiary upon death (GMDB), a minimum lump sum to be withdrawn at a given point in the future (GMAB), a minimum level at which the assets will be converted into an annuity income stream with the guaranteed conversion rate (GMIB) or a minimum level of guaranteed withdrawals from the investment account to be taken as annuity income during the drawdown phase (GMWB/GLWB). The level of guarantee may be defined in advance or depend on market performance.

These optional types of guarantees which can be offered with variable annuities are summarised here:

- *Guaranteed Minimum Death Benefit (GMDB)* – Guarantees a minimum sum to be paid to beneficiaries upon death; the amount paid will be the maximum of the actual account value or the guaranteed value.
- *Guaranteed Minimum Accumulation Benefit (GMAB)* – Guarantees a minimum return on assets for the purpose of taking a lump sum withdrawal from the product at a specified future date; the amount paid will be the maximum of the actual account value or the guaranteed value.
- *Guaranteed Minimum Income Benefit (GMIB)* – Guarantees a minimum rate of return on investment during the accumulation/deferral phase for the calculation of the conversion of the accumulated funds into a fixed annuity, effectively guaranteeing a minimum level of income from the future annuity payments. The guaranteed level of income will vary by the age at which the annuity payments begin.
- *Guaranteed Minimum Lifetime Withdrawal Benefit (GLWB)* – Guarantees a minimum level of withdrawals, typically defined as a percentage of the guarantee level, which in some cases has the potential to continue to increase in the event that the account value grows. This benefit allows continued participation in market returns during the drawdown phase without requiring full annuitisation, and can guarantee withdrawals over a specified number of years (GMWB) or for life (GLWB) even if the account value falls to zero. The latter provides longevity protection as a life annuity would, albeit with a lower guaranteed income level. The guaranteed level of income will vary by the age at which payments begin.

The guarantee levels themselves can be defined in advance or based on actual investment performance, and typically take one or more of the following forms (Geneva Association, 2013):

- *Roll-ups* – A guaranteed annual return of a specified rate, e.g. 4%
- *Ratchets* – Guarantees that accumulated assets will never decrease from the value assessed at pre-defined intervals, e.g. annually
- *Resets* – Equivalent to ratchets except the time at which the value is assessed is determined by the policyholder (within limits)

Based on the guarantee(s) provided, an explicit fee will be regularly deducted from the value of the account to cover the expected cost of the guarantee in addition to a fee for administering the product. The fees, however, do not reduce the level of the guarantee. Some contracts also offer a no-lapse guarantee, where the contract and guarantees will remain in place even if the account value drops to zero during the accumulation phase, as long as the individual has not withdrawn amounts over the prescribed limits.

These guarantees could become quite valuable for the annuitant during market downturns, such as during the financial crisis. Figure 3.2 illustrates the hypothetical value of such guarantees compared to the actual investment performance of an account. The intrinsic value of the guarantee, or the extent to which it is 'in-the-money', is represented by the difference between the guaranteed level (either the 4% rollup or the annual ratchet) over the actual account value. In the illustration below based on a contract beginning in 1998 and invested in the S&P 500, both guarantees were significantly above the actual account value in 2009 (the value of the original investment accumulated at the S&P 500 annual returns), meaning the guarantees were 'in-the-money'. The level of the guarantee for the annual ratchet is based on the maximum value the account had reached in the past (in this case the value of the account in 2007) and for the 4% rollup is based on achieving an annual return each year of 4%. If the annuity provider was obliged to make payments to the annuitant in 2009 for example based on the guaranteed value, it would have had to make up any shortfall of the account value with funds coming from its general account.

Figure 3.2. **Illustration of guarantee forms**

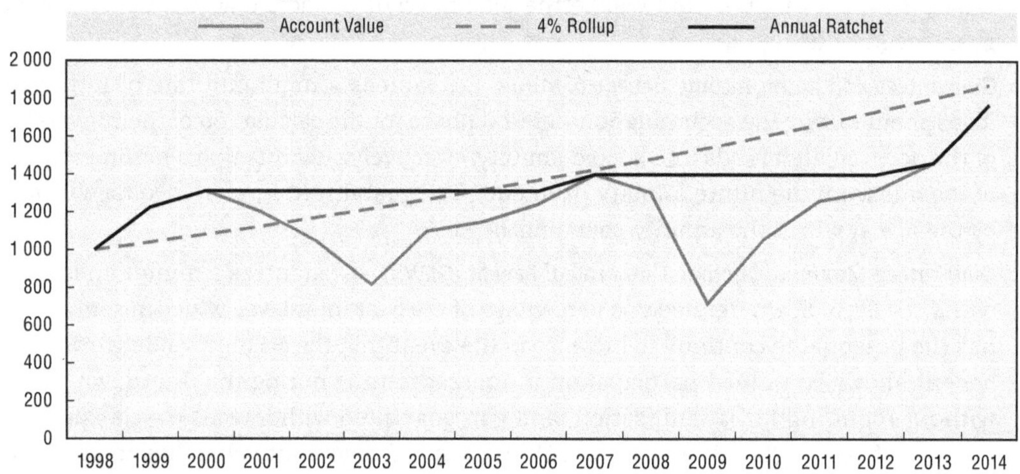

Note: The value in the first year is set to 1000 and then the different annual returns (market, rollup, annual ratchet) are applied in successive years.
Source: Based on a contract beginning in 1998 and invested in the S&P 500.

Given these product features, the main risks faced by the annuity provider are related to market risks, longevity/mortality, and consumer behaviour. Market risk exposure is primarily driven by the exposure to equity and interest rates from the assets in which the contract is invested. Longevity/mortality and behaviour risks are inter-related with market risks as the value of the guarantees and payments made are a function of the underlying account value and are sensitive to timing.

Product design features can drive the risk exposure of the annuity provider for each of these risks, with the design of the guarantee(s) offered, the underlying asset portfolios and the options provided to the annuitant all influencing the overall level of risk. The main risks to which variable annuities are exposed to, their drivers and the ways in which product design can be used to control the level of risk exposure, are summarised in Table 3.2.

Table 3.2. **Risk exposures from variable annuity product design**

Risk Type	Risk Drivers	Risk management tools through product design
Mortality/longevity	Mortality/Longevity	Age limits
		Natural hedge in guarantees offered
		Risk Pooling
Investment	Asset allocation	Limit number of funds
		Automatic rebalancing and/or volatility caps
	Fees	Linked to equity exposure or volatility
		Based on guarantee level vs. account value
	Level of guarantee	Control timing and frequency of resets and/or level of rollup
Behavioural	Timing/choice of annuitisation	Age and timing limits
	Fund Switching	Limit frequency/available funds
	Surrender	Surrender penalties
	Dollar-for-dollar vs. pro-rata withdrawals	Limit dollar-for-dollar

The inclusion and design of the guarantees play an important role in the risk exposure of the annuity provider and the probability that the guarantee will eventually be 'in-the-money'. The first consideration is the nature of the guarantee and the risk it is insuring. For the basic guarantee, the annuity provider guarantees the rate at which accumulated assets can be converted into an annuity. The additional optional guarantees offer additional protection against investment and/or longevity/mortality risks.

The basic guarantee, which is a guaranteed annuity conversion rate, provides a combination of investment and longevity protection at a future point in time. This conversion rate locks in the discount rate and mortality assumptions which can be used for the conversion of the accumulated assets into an annuity at the time of issue of the annuity contract. If no additional investment guarantees are elected, the individual bears full investment risk during the accumulation period, and this conversion rate would be applied to the actual value of the assets accumulated in the account.

For the basic guarantee, the annuity provider faces the behavioural risk that the annuitant will convert his assets into an annuity at the end of the accumulation period when the guarantee is 'in-the-money'. If at the time of conversion interest rates are lower than the discount rate which was locked in or longevity expectations are significantly higher, the prevailing cost to purchase a new annuity would be higher than that guaranteed rate and the guarantee would therefore be 'in-the-money'. The individual would then benefit from annuitising their assets, with the annuity provider having to make up the difference in cost. The longer the accumulation/deferral period of the contract, the greater the risk that this guaranteed annuity option will be 'in-the-money' (because of an increase in longevity and/or a decrease in interest rates) and thereby costly to the annuity provider if the annuity option is exercised. As a result age limits may be imposed both for the issue age and the ages at which assets can be annuitised in order to limit some of this longevity and behavioural risk exposure.

Mortality and/or longevity risk exposure also arises for the optional guarantees offered for which payments are contingent on survival. The payment of the GMDB guarantee is dependent on the death of the individual during the accumulation phase and therefore the valuation of this guarantee must take mortality assumptions into account. If the guarantee is 'in-the-money' at the time the payment is owed, that is the guaranteed value of the payment is greater than the actual account value, the annuity provider will have to make up the difference. The GMIB and GLWB guarantees expose the annuity provider to longevity risk as payments are promised for the lifetime of the individual, and therefore they must also account for mortality assumptions in their valuation. To partially mitigate this longevity risk, the annuity provider can incorporate a natural hedge in the product line by offering both the GMDB and GMIB/GLWB as mortality risk from the GMDB could partially offset longevity risk from the GMIB/GLWBs.

While the GMIB and GLWBs are both exposed to longevity risk, the nature of their exposures is not identical. The longevity risk exposure for a GMIB is similar to that of other types of annuities in the case of annuitisation, as if the annuitisation option is utilised, the accumulated assets are relinquished to the annuity provider to be converted into a fixed annuity. As such, the longevity risk for these types of guarantees can be reduced through the pooling of a large number of annuitants.

However, the proportion of individuals with a GMIB who actually elect to annuitise tends to be quite low, and has remained so even given the recent market turmoil and the higher probability that their guarantee has been 'in-the-money' (SOA and LIMRA, 2013). This is likely due to the same reasons that explain why traditional annuities are unpopular, one of those reasons being the reluctance of individuals to give up access to their assets or underlying funds. This trend has so far limited the actual longevity exposure that annuity providers face from these guarantees.

In contrast to the GMIB, the GLWB does not benefit from the same level of longevity risk pooling, and for this guarantee the annuity provider remains exposed to the surrender behaviour risk. This is because the annuitant retains access to the underlying assets, with any remaining assets in the account being paid to the annuitant's beneficiary upon death. Furthermore the annuitant may also surrender the policy and withdraw all assets if the guarantee provided is no longer valuable to him, though penalties may apply. As a result the guaranteed level of income will generally be lower than the guaranteed level under a GMIB given similar investment guarantees so as to remain actuarially neutral and account for the lower level of longevity risk pooling.

In addition to the definition of how payments are triggered, other design aspects also play an important role in the risk exposures resulting from the guarantees. These aspects include how the assets are invested, how the investment strategy can be changed over time, the frequency and timing at which the level of the guarantee is updated, the ability for the policyholder to withdraw funds, the duration and amount of surrender charges and the flexibility provided around the time at which the drawdown phase of the product may begin.

The underlying asset allocation clearly influences the risk exposure of the annuity provider when guarantees are offered. The individual generally has a choice of how to invest the premium for a variable annuity contract, and can select from several investment funds offered by the annuity provider. The risk profile of the selected investment funds themselves and how these investments are changed over time can impact the value of the guarantees offered and therefore the risk that they fall 'in-the-money'.

Funds with a higher risk profile imply a higher cost of any guarantee offered, since the fund's return would be subject to more volatility and would have a higher likelihood of falling below any guaranteed return. Limiting the number of funds available can allow the annuity provider to better control the risk profile of the investments and increase the effectiveness of its hedging strategy for investment risks going forward (which will be discussed in the next section). Automatic asset allocation may also be implemented by the provider to better control the investment risk exposure, for example by rebalancing the portfolio between equities and fixed-income or ensuring that the fund does not exceed a certain volatility threshold (volatility caps).

The level of fees charged can be designed to compensate the annuity provider for the additional risk from investing in higher risk funds. Generally each guarantee provided by the product incurs a fee defined as a fixed percentage of the underlying value. However, this percentage may vary by fund depending on the fund's equity exposure or volatility, as these features present additional risk to the annuity provider and make the guarantees more valuable. Additionally, fees can be applied to the level of the guarantee rather than the underlying asset value in order to avoid decreased fee income when markets are also performing poorly and the guarantee is more valuable.

The annuity provider may also be exposed to behavioural risk where the individual is given the option to change the asset allocation over time (fund-switching) which can also increase the costs and risk of providing guarantees. Frequent trading increases trading costs and makes the risk profile of the investments potentially less stable, presenting a challenge for the annuity provider to hedge its investment risk. As a result, the annuity provider may limit the frequency or extent to which investments can be changed in order to limit the risk exposure.

The way in which the guarantee level is designed to be updated will impact the risk exposure and the cost of providing the guarantee as well. The risk that the guarantee will be 'in-the-money' at any given point in time is increased where more frequent updates or more control of the timing of updates by the individual are allowed. The higher the frequency with which the ratchet guarantee is updated, the higher the risk that the guarantee will be higher than the account value at any given point in time and therefore the higher the risk exposure to the annuity provider. Similarly, if the annuitant is given the option to select the timing at which the level of guarantees is reset, they will more likely select to reset when markets are at their highest, also increasing the probability that the guarantee will be 'in-the-money' at any given point in time. The fees charged for more frequent and flexible updating of the guarantee would therefore increase accordingly.

In addition to the extent to which the individual can opt to reset his guarantee or change their investment allocation, the annuity provider can be exposed to several other behavioural risks which increase its overall risk exposure. Behavioural risks come into play wherever flexibility is offered in the product and depend on the choices the individual makes. Flexibility around the timing that the drawdown phase begins and the ability for the individual to withdraw funds from the policy are main drivers of behavioural risk. Generally speaking, the more predictable the behaviour is, the less risk there is to the annuity provider. Product design features which increase the predictability of behaviour are therefore the main way to control the annuity provider's exposure to behavioural risks.

The timing at which income from the GMIB guarantee begins impacts the value of the guarantee and therefore the risk exposure of the annuity provider. As previously mentioned, the individual will likely not benefit from converting their assets into an annuity at the end of the accumulation period if the annuity guarantee is not in-the-money. Therefore the risk exposure to the annuity provider depends greatly on the timing of the conversion. The greater the difference is between the account value and the guaranteed value when the annuity option is elected, the more expensive the annuity is for the provider. As consumers are more likely to choose to annuitise when the option is more valuable to them, this timing can be modelled dynamically as a function of the value of the guarantee. Age limits or constraints on the timing (e.g. only at contract anniversaries) reduces some of the uncertainty of this option and therefore also reduces some of the risk exposure for the annuity provider.

The time at which the individual begins withdrawing funds under a GLWB also matters. Generally, the earlier the withdrawals commence, the larger the risk that the account value will be depleted before the individual dies and that the annuity provider will have to pay out additional payments. Furthermore if the guaranteed level is above the account value when withdrawals begin, the risk that the account will be depleted is much larger. Again age limits or constraints regarding the timing that drawdown begins can help to mitigate this risk.

The ability for the individual to withdraw funds from their account or fully surrender the policy also poses a behavioural risk to the annuity provider. Surrender charges are generally imposed during the first several years of the contract as a penalty for early surrenders in order to cover any upfront costs that the annuity provider incurred by issuing the contract. Therefore in optimising their surrender behaviour, individuals will consider the value of keeping the guarantees in the contract compared to the account value net of surrender charges. If investment returns have been poor and the guarantee is more valuable, the individual will be less likely to surrender. This implies that these types of guarantees are counter-cyclical in that annuity providers face less liquidity risk in poor economic environments because the policyholders will keep their money in the contract. Nevertheless in these scenarios, the value of the liabilities can also significantly increase, exposing the annuity provider to the risk of lower rates of surrender than expected as liabilities would then be higher than expected.

The risk that withdrawals pose to the annuity provider depends in part on how the withdrawals impact the guarantee value. Any partial withdrawals from the account (excluding guaranteed withdrawal benefits) will reduce the level of the guarantee. However this can be done in one of two ways: either dollar-for-dollar, meaning that for each dollar withdrawn the guarantee is also reduced by a dollar, or pro-rata, where the guarantee reduced by the equivalent proportion of assets which are withdrawn.

Dollar-for-dollar withdrawals expose the annuity provider to more risk compared to pro-rata withdrawals. To illustrate why this is so, consider a simple case where the contract has a GMAB currently valued at 500, but the account value is only at 400. In other words the guarantee is worth 100. If the individual can withdraw funds dollar-for-dollar, he can withdraw 300 leaving 100 in the account and reducing the guarantee level by the amount withdrawn, from 500 to 200. The guarantee is still valued at 100 (the guarantee level of 200 minus the account value of 100). However, the assets backing the guarantee now represent only 50% of the liabilities rather than 80% of the liabilities which was initially the case. With a pro-rata withdrawal, the guarantee level would be reduced by the proportion of cash withdrawn compared to the account value, or in other words by 75% to 125, and the assets in the account would still cover 80% of the liability. As a result of the higher risk exposure to the annuity provider, the amount that an individual can withdraw dollar-for-dollar is generally more limited.

The behaviour which maximises the risk to the annuity provider is the behaviour which will maximise the liability value of the contract and therefore maximise its economic utility to the individual. In other words an individual who exercises options and elects to receive benefits at times when the guarantees are the most valuable presents a higher risk to the annuity provider. However assuming perfectly rational behaviour can make such guarantees prohibitively expensive. While annuity providers do seem to implement some level of dynamism in their behaviour assumptions and link them to the guarantee value, annuity providers seem to be pricing the guarantees allowing for some level of irrationality. This also means, however, that the annuity providers are exposed to a larger risk that behaviour will be more rational than expected, and therefore that their liabilities will increase (Kling et al., 2014).

Counterintuitively, the annuity provider's exposure to behavioural risk can be lower with more costly guarantees, as these guarantees are more likely to be in the money at any given point in time, thereby rendering surrender behaviour more predictable (i.e. the surrender rate could be assumed to be very low if not zero). Kling et al. (2014) demonstrated this for the case of GLWBs. Nevertheless, more costly guarantees are generally exposed to a larger level of investment risk, so there is a trade-off between the two.

Management of risk exposures for variable annuities

The main risk to manage for variable annuities going forward is the market risk related to the guarantees offered. Unlike insurance risks, investment risks are not diversifiable through pooling; if equity markets perform poorly or interest rates drop, this will have a negative impact on the entire portfolio of contracts. The investment risk management for these products is significantly more challenging than for other types of annuity products due to the dynamic nature of the guarantees, the variety of investment funds into which assets are allocated and the interaction of market risks with both the insurance and behaviour risks. This complexity necessitates a more comprehensive risk management strategy for the investment risks faced by the annuity provider.

The main market risks variable annuity providers face are a fall in equity markets, a decrease in interest rates and an increase in market volatility. Each of these drivers increases the value of the guarantees provided and therefore increases the liability value. If left unhedged, the annuity provider is exposed to the risk that it will experience an increase in its liability value, which is likely to be accompanied by a decrease in its asset base, negatively impacting its earnings and solvency position. If the annuity provider hedges these risks correctly, an increase in the liability value due to these drivers would instead be offset by an increase on the asset side, allowing the annuity provider to maintain its earnings level and solvency position.

The table below summarizes the approaches to managing market risks for variable annuities along with their benefits and disadvantages.[9]

Table 3.3. **Hedging strategies for variable annuities**

Hedging Strategy	Pros	Cons
None	Fully profit from positive market movements	High capital requirements, large tail risks
OTC static hedge	Effective in matching liability value, no need for frequent rebalancing	Expensive, credit risk, illiquid, transaction times
Dynamic hedging	Potentially less expensive, flexible	Resource intensive, basis risk, transaction costs, less effective in tumultuous markets

The first option the annuity provider is to not hedge its investment risks at all. However, the tails of the distributions of the risks to which variable annuities are exposed can be quite large, requiring a significant level of capital to ensure the solvency of the annuity provider if these risks are not explicitly hedged and/or mitigated. Given the cost of holding such high levels of capital and the significant downside risk, most variable annuity providers hedge the guarantees they offer using derivative instruments in order to protect themselves from negative market movements and to smooth earnings volatility.

Hedging these risks typically requires only a fraction of the capital which would otherwise be necessary to cover the risk and greatly reduces the tail risk faced by the annuity provider, though hedging also reduces the annuity providers' potential gain in good markets. The annuity provider has two main options to hedge its investment risk: using an over-the-counter (OTC) hedge which is tailored specifically to its products' profile, or dynamically hedge its risk using exchange traded derivatives.

The best hedge for the annuity provider would be to invest in an asset which matches the expected cash flows of the guarantee. The guarantees embedded in variable annuity products are essentially put options on the underlying account value, meaning that the annuity provider is selling the individual the option to sell the assets in his account at a certain price (the strike price), which in this case is the guarantee level. Therefore if the annuity provider could purchase a matching put option, this could hedge the underlying guarantee. Box 3.1 provides a description of the basic types of options (plain vanilla) which can be traded on exchanges.[10]

Box 3.1. **Definitions of plain vanilla options**

European put option: Gives the owner the right to sell the underlying asset at the strike price at the maturity date of the option. If the asset value is lower than the strike price at the expiration of the option, the owner will benefit from the difference.

American put option: Equivalent to the European put option, except the owner has the right to sell the underlying asset at the strike price at any point until the maturity date of the option.

European call option: Gives the owner the right to buy the underlying asset at the strike price at the maturity date of the option. If the asset value is higher than the strike price at the expiration of the option, the owner will benefit from having an asset valued at more than what he paid.

American call option: Equivalent to the European call option, except the owner has the right to buy the underlying asset at the strike price at any point until the maturity date of the option.

However, put options matching variable annuity guarantees are not readily available on the exchange market, and the annuity provider would have to purchase an over-the-counter (OTC) option to better match the duration and strike price characteristics of the put option it has shorted. OTC options, however, can be relatively expensive, are less liquid, and involve a higher level of credit risk and much longer transaction times compared to exchange traded options.

Exchange traded options do not perfectly match the variable annuity guarantees for several reasons. First, exchange traded options are typically of a very short duration and not appropriate for the long duration of a variable annuity contract. In addition, the strike price of the option provided by the guarantee changes over time as the guarantee level increases, and the time at which this option can be exercised varies.

The alternative to hedging with an OTC contract then is that the annuity provider uses dynamic hedging and approximates the option with more standardised derivative instruments traded on exchanges. This requires the annuity provider to have an asset portfolio which mimics the sensitivity of the liability value to small changes in each of the risk drivers.

The sensitivities of the liabilities to changes in risk drivers are commonly referred to by their Greek symbols: delta (Δ) is the sensitivity to changes in the price of the underlying fund, gamma (γ) is a second order risk driven by the convexity of the liabilities and represents the sensitivity of delta to changes in the underlying fund, rho (ρ) is the sensitivity to the change in interest rates and vega (ν) is the sensitivity to the change in implied volatility.

Table 3.4 summarises these market risks and the types of derivatives which are typically used to hedge them.

Table 3.4. **Risks hedged for variable annuities**

Greek	Definition	Derivative instruments commonly used to hedge
Delta	Liabilities' sensitivity to changes in the underlying asset (e.g. equity)	Futures on equity indices
Gamma	Convexity of the liabilities, i.e. the sensitivity of delta to changes in the underlying asset	Call/put options on equity indices
Rho	Liabilities' sensitivity to changes in interest rates	Interest rate swaps
Vega	Liabilities' sensitivity to changes in implied volatility	Equity options, interest rate options, swaptions

Delta hedging against movements in the underlying fund value is the most common hedging strategy implemented by variable annuity providers. The main instruments employed for delta hedging are exchange traded future contracts, which specify the price at which the owner of the future will buy the underlying asset at some point in the future, and which can be transacted at a very low cost. These contracts are generally marked to market daily, so the annuity provider will have to put up an initial reserve plus a maintenance reserve to cover the cash settlements as prices fluctuate.

Delta hedging for equity risk typically relies on exchanged traded futures on equity indices. The primary way annuity providers implement this type of hedge is to short futures on an equity index, meaning that it agrees to sell the shares at a given price in the future. Therefore if the price of equities falls, it will still be able to sell the shares at the higher price agreed in the future contract. The amount of futures that the annuity provider will need to offset the increase in liabilities from a decrease in equity prices depends on the sensitivity of the liability value to equity movements. If the liability value increases by 10 000 following a 1% decrease in the S&P Index, for example, the annuity provider could short 10 000 worth of S&P futures, and if the index falls by 1% it will receive a payment to offset the increase in liability value.

Delta hedges are generally effective for small movements in the index being hedged. This effectiveness, however, can be greatly reduced for larger movements as the liability value also depends on other factors such as interest rates, volatility, mortality assumptions and even surrender assumptions, and therefore does not follow a linear sensitivity to changes in the equity index. If any of these underlying variables change, the liability value changes as does its sensitivity to equity movements. The sensitivity of delta is known as gamma, and represents the change in the delta calculation due to the convexity of the liabilities.

This relationship between the annuity liabilities and the payoff from the delta hedge is demonstrated in Figure 3.3. The point at which the hedge payoff is tangent to the liability value is the point at which the delta for the hedge should be calculated. For large movements in the underlying index, it is clear that the hedge payoff will not match the change in liability value. Here, the difference between the liability value and the hedge payoff is essentially the cost of the hedge. Because of the convexity, the delta hedge will never be perfect; the larger the movement in the underlying index is, the higher the incurred hedging costs.

Figure 3.3. **Illustration of delta hedging**

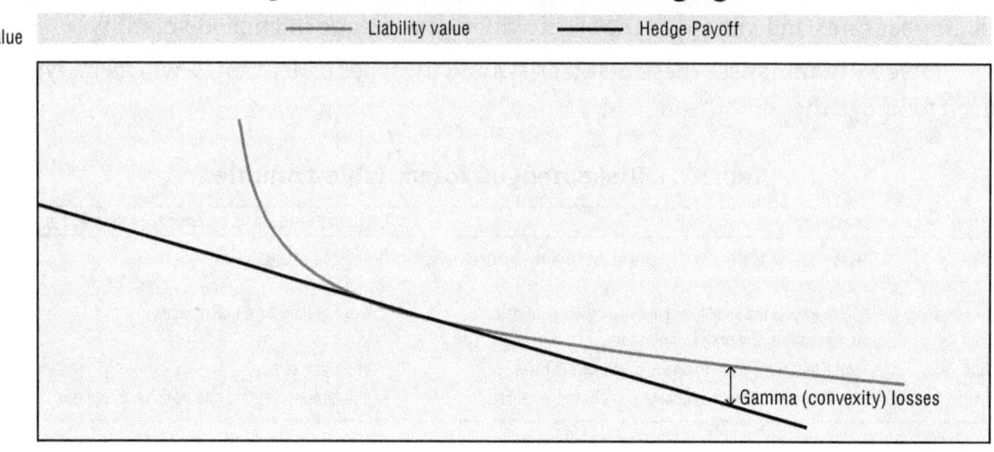

The sensitivity of delta to the change in the liability value necessitates that the delta hedge be frequently rebalanced. The annuity provider typically will define this frequency along with the thresholds which would require rebalancing, and if the liabilities only change by a small amount the costs of rebalancing the hedge likely outweigh the benefits. There is a direct trade-off between frequent rebalancing to maintain the hedge's effectiveness and the increased transaction costs incurred.

While frequently rebalancing the delta hedge reduces exposure to gamma risk, the risk does remain that the underlying asset will experience a large shock and the delta will change dramatically, resulting in significant hedging losses. This is a second order risk driven by the convexity of the liabilities. As protection against this risk, the annuity provider could also hedge the gamma risk, or in other words it could hedge the sensitivity of delta. This involves the purchase of additional options for which the payoff structure would offset the losses from movements in the underlying asset. Once the appropriate gamma hedge has been determined, the delta hedge would need to be rebalanced to maintain neutrality. Gamma hedging clearly increases the expense and complexity of the hedging strategy, and is generally only implemented for annuity providers with extensive hedging programs.

After delta hedging, annuity providers also commonly hedge against the movements in interest rates, referred to as rho hedging. As with fixed annuities, variable annuities are also exposed to decreasing interest rates coming from two sources: the potential for lower future returns due to reinvestment risk and the increased economic value of the liabilities. This latter risk is more complicated than for fixed annuities, however, as the level of interest rates directly impacts the value of the put option which the guarantee represents, making the economic value of variable annuities more sensitive to interest rate movements. Interest rate swaps, discussed in the section on risk management for fixed payment annuities, can be used to hedge interest rate risk for these products.

The impact of volatility risk and the way in which it is mitigated depends on the type of volatility considered. The source of volatility risk can come from either realised volatility, which is the actual observed volatility of assets, or the implied volatility (vega), which is inferred from observed option prices.

An increase in realised volatility will increase the gamma losses to the extent that gamma is not hedged. This is because higher volatility results in larger movements of the asset which is delta hedged, significantly reducing hedge effectiveness. Risk stemming from realised volatility can be controlled through gamma hedging and/or imposing volatility caps or automatic rebalancing of the underlying funds.

An increase in implied volatility (vega) increases both the liability value and the hedging costs. Increased implied volatility directly impacts the value of the put options from the guarantees resulting in an increase in economic liabilities. Furthermore, an increase in implied volatility implies an increase in the cost of the options used to hedge the liabilities, so rolling forward the hedge positions will result in higher hedging transaction costs. Vega is typically hedged using equity or interest rate options to offset the change in liability value due to a change in implied volatility. However this sensitivity is less commonly hedged compared to delta and rho due to its complexity and expense, and as with gamma must be done in conjunction with determining the appropriate delta hedge.

As the hedging strategy is based on the sensitivity of the liabilities to equity, interest rate and volatility movements, it is forcibly dependent on the definition of the liability measurement. The liability measurement targeted for the hedging strategy will depend on the objectives of hedging, as results will differ to the extent that accounting, statutory and economic measures of the liabilities differ. Targeting the GAAP accounting measure of liabilities will be more effective for smoothing earnings volatility, but will leave the economic liabilities under-hedged. Statutory measures of the liability are somewhat more sensitive to the risk drivers than the GAAP accounting measures, particularly to equity movements, though the under-hedging of interest rates can result and the hedge will still not be appropriate in economic terms. Hedging the economic liabilities results in hedging which most accurately offsets the true fair market value of the liabilities, though tends to be more expensive than hedging the other bases (Geneva Association, 2013). Annuity providers may have less incentive to hedge liabilities which are not measured at fair value for accounting purposes as the benefits from hedging may not be fully reflected in earnings (Chopra et al, 2009).

Hedging programs have proven to be a valuable risk management tool for variable annuity providers, and were estimated to save the industry USD 40 billion at the onset of the financial crisis in 2008. However hedging programs faced numerous challenges during these tumultuous times, leading these hedging strategies to be less effective than they were under normal market conditions. These inefficiencies cost the industry USD 4 billion during the same period, September and October of 2008 (Chopra et al, 2009).

The reduction in the effectiveness of the hedging strategies of variable annuity providers during the financial crises was a result of several interconnected drivers. First was the increase of basis risk, or the mismatch between the hedge and the change in the liability value. Delta hedging strategies rely primarily on the purchase of futures on equity indices, whereas the variable annuity contracts can be invested in a variety of investment funds. To the extent that these investments do not track with the equity index used for hedging, the hedge will not perfectly offset the losses from the investment funds. The difference between the index performance and the actual investment performance results in losses due to basis risk, and this divergence increased during the crisis.

Secondly was the increased cost of the derivative instruments used to hedge. Increased volatility of the market reached historical highs during this period. As mentioned earlier, an increase in implied volatility can significantly impact the cost of the options used to hedge risks. Additionally, this increased volatility was accompanied by increased credit spreads and illiquidity, pushing the option costs even higher.

The increased volatility also led to challenges with respect to the timing of the rebalancing of the dynamic hedging strategies. Rebalancing became difficult because of the large market swings. If the hedge was rebalanced following a drop in the market which subsequently bounced back, for example, large hedging losses could result.

Finally, the market turmoil resulted in surrender behaviour which was not in line with expectations. Because the guarantees of the variable annuity products became more valuable, individuals tended to hold on to their contracts in order to keep these guarantees, resulting in higher total liabilities than planned for. As such the liability being hedged was different from the actual liability, resulting in additional losses.

Operational risk can also be an issue for variable annuity products given the complexity involved and continued monitoring and rebalancing which is necessary. Dedicated resources in terms of both human capital and computing resources are necessary to implement these types of hedging programs. Appropriate processes and controls must therefore be put in place to mitigate operational risk. The necessary level of specialised knowledge, technical infrastructure and deep and liquid capital markets needed to implement these types of programs would be a barrier for these types of products to be offered in many markets.

Risk management of fixed [equity] indexed annuities

Risks from the product design and assumptions of fixed indexed annuities

Fixed indexed annuity products are somewhat of a cross between a fixed annuity and a variable annuity. These products offer a minimum guaranteed return on investment, potential for additional investment growth, access to the underlying funds and the option for minimum guaranteed withdrawal benefits.

The individual typically has a few limited options as to how their funds are invested and how the interest on his premium will be credited by the annuity provider. Generally an option to receive a credited level of interest with no indexation, indexation based on one or more equity indices or a combination of these is offered. The indexed options offer a low guaranteed minimum rate of return of 0-2%, and usually impose a participation rate (e.g. 75% of the index's return) and/or a cap on the level of the index return which can be credited to the individual. The cap on annual return is typically around 4-5%, and dividends are usually excluded from the calculation of the credited return. Variations on this type of product, such as structured-note annuities, allow for a more customised return profile and increased investment risk sharing, with the consumer potentially bearing some of the downside risk.

There are typically three ways for index returns to be credited annually to the individual's account subject to any caps imposed:

- *Point-to-point* – the realised return over the entire year
- *Monthly average* – the monthly realised return averaged over the whole year
- *Monthly sum cap* – the sum of all monthly returns subject to the relevant caps

If the calculated index return falls below the minimum guaranteed credited rate, the minimum rate is credited to the account.

The individual maintains access to the underlying assets and is allowed to make withdrawals, although surrender penalties may apply and withdrawals over a certain level could affect the guaranteed level of the account.

As with variable annuities, guaranteed withdrawal benefits are also now commonly offered over a certain term or for life for a fee which is deducted from the account value. This guaranteed level can also have the potential to increase over time along with market returns. Some products also offer options for early withdrawals without penalty given certain circumstances, such as a terminal illness or to cover long-term care.

Given the limits imposed regarding the choice of indices and the cap on the indexed return which is credited, this product design presents less market risk to the annuity provider than variable annuities. As the annuity provider is not obliged to pass all of the positive returns on to the individual in good markets, those funds can go to cover the minimum guaranteed return in periods of poor market returns, or alternatively to cover hedging costs. This means that the fees charged to the contract should also be lower than those for a variable annuity.

Behaviour risk exposure is also likely to be lower than for variable annuities, since the investment guarantees are likely to be less valuable given the limits on participation in the index return. Therefore the annuity provider will not risk losing as much in the event that the individual surrenders or withdraws from their policy. Nevertheless, surrender behaviour which differs from what is assumed will have an impact on the effectiveness of the investment hedging strategy implemented, and does present a certain degree of liquidity risk for the annuity provider. Surrender risk is mitigated through the surrender charges imposed in the product design.

Longevity risk exposure from the GLWB offered is similar to that of the variable annuity.

Management of risk exposures for fixed indexed annuities

As with variable annuities, the main risk that annuity providers are able to manage going forward is the investment risk related to the level of guaranteed returns and any GLWB offered. For a basic fixed indexed annuity the hedging strategy is relatively straightforward. The annuity provider can invest in fixed income instruments to cover the minimum guaranteed return and implement dynamic delta hedging with call options on the equity index in order to participate in market gains. With a call option, if the index exceeds the strike price, the annuity provider will receive the difference to cover the indexed return participation to the individual. Furthermore, the basis risk of this strategy would be more limited than for a variable annuity as the options would be based on the same index as the interest credited to the contract. As these call options should be available on exchanges, the additional credit risk to the annuity provider from using these instruments would also be limited.

Generally speaking, the higher the level of the guarantees offered by the product and the greater the level of flexibility, the higher the level of risk exposure to the annuity provider. There is therefore a trade-off between higher levels of security and flexibility for the consumer and the complexity of the tools needed to manage the resulting risk exposures from the product. Policy makers will need to ensure that the appropriate framework is in place to ensure that the products developed to meet society's needs are sustainable and encourage the annuity providers to manage their risks appropriately. These issues which drive the availability and design of annuity products will be discussed in the following chapter.

Notes

1. See the IAA Risk Book for a more thorough discussion of the different aspects of risk management. *www.actuaries.org/LIBRARY/Papers/RiskBookChapters/IAA_Risk_Book_Iceberg_Cover_and_ToC_25May2016.pdf.*
2. The 2014 OECD report *Mortality Assumptions and Longevity Risk: Implications For Pension Funds and Annuity Providers* (OECD, 2014) provides a discussion on the management of longevity risk. It advises that pension funds and annuity providers use regularly updated mortality tables which include future improvements in mortality for valuing annuity and pension liabilities. It also provides a discussion of capital market solutions to mitigate longevity risk.
3. This assumes that government bonds are considered to be a risk-free investment, which may not always technically be the case.
4. See the *OECD Business and Finance Outlook 2015*, (OECD, 2015) Chapter 4, "Can pension funds and life insurance companies keep their promises?"
5. The discussion herein follows OECD (2014), *Mortality Assumptions and Longevity Risk: Implications for Pension Funds and Annuity Providers.*
6. Based on calculations for a US female assuming a discount rate of 4.5%.
7. Rocha et al (2011) refer to these types of products as 'extendable annuities'.
8. Other types of insurance products may be exposed to anti-selection risk at the issue of the contract or to the amount and timing of premium payments made during the accumulation phase, but the options that the annuitant has beyond this are quite limited. Surrender risk may exist for some other products as well, but in general there is less flexibility allowed for withdrawals and therefore less behavioural risk for other types of products.
9. Reinsurance has not been considered as a strategy here as these solutions are not widely available and are very expensive, though reinsurance can be used cost effectively in group sales where guaranteed issue is required.
10. European options are more commonly traded on exchanges.

References

Chopra, D. et al. (2009), "Responding to the Variable Annuity Crisis", *McKinsey Working Papers on Risk*, No. 10, McKinsey & Company.

The Geneva Association (2013), "Variable Annuities – An Analysis of Financial Stability", Geneva.

Ji, M., M. Hardy, J. Li (2012), "Markovian Approaches to Joint-life Mortality", University of Waterloo, Ontario.

Johnson, N. (2000), "Martial Status and Mortality: The National Longitudinal Mortality Study", *Annals of Epidemiology*, Volume 10, Issue 4, May 2000, pp224-238.

Kling, A., A. Richter, J. Ruß (2007), "The interaction of guarantees, surplus distribution, and asset allocation in with-profit life insurance policies", *Insurance: Mathematics and Economics* 40, pp 164-178.

Kling, A., F. Ruez, J. Ruß (2014), "The impact of policyholder behaviour on pricing, hedging and hedge efficiency of withdrawal benefit guarantees in variable annuities", *European Actuarial Journal*, Vol. 4, Issue 2, pp 281-314, DOI: 10.1007/s13385-014-0093-0.

Maurer, R. et al. (2014), "Accounting and Actuarial smoothing of Retirement Payouts in Participating Life Annuities", National Bureau of Economic Research, Working Paper 20124, Cambridge.

Milevsky, M. (2002), "How to completely avoid outliving your money: An introduction to variable payout annuities for retiring Canadians", Toronto.

OECD (2015), *OECD Business and Finance Outlook 2015*, OECD Publishing, Paris, *http://dx.doi.org/10.1787/9789264234291-en.*

OECD (2014), *Mortality Assumptions and Longevity Risk: Implications for pension funds and annuity providers*, OECD Publishing, Paris, *http://dx.doi.org/10.1787/9789264222748-en*.

Rocha, R., D. Vittas, H. P. Rudolph (2011), "Annuities and Other Retirement Products: Designing the Payout Phase", World Bank, Washington D.C.

Society of Actuaries, LIMRA (2013), "Variable Annuity Guaranteed Living Benefit Utilization: 2011 Experience", Society of Actuaries and LL Global, Inc.

Spreeuw, J., I. Owadally (2013), Investigating the Broken-Heart Effect: a Model for Short-Term Dependence between the Remaining Lifetimes of Joint Lives. Annals of Actuarial Science, 7, pp 236-257 doi:10.1017/S1748499512000292.

Tiong, S. (2013), "Pricing inflation-linked variable annuities under stochastic interest rates", *Insurance: Mathematics and Economics* 52, pp. 77-86 doi:10.1016/j.insmatheco.2012.11.003.

Chapter 4

Drivers of annuity product availability, design and sustainability

This chapter discusses three main drivers of annuity product design and availability: direct or indirect constraints within the context of the pension system; consumer demand for the product; and the sustainability of the product given the risks presented and the regulatory requirements in place. It draws on the experiences of different markets as examples. This discussion highlights the issues that policy makers should consider when putting in place a framework to ensure that the most essential aspects of annuity product design are given priority and to encourage the development of sustainable products which will adequately meet consumers' needs.

Annuity product design is shaped by three key drivers: direct or indirect constraints within the context of the pension system, consumer demand for the product, and the sustainability of the product given the risks presented and the regulatory requirements in place. In other words, the product has to be designed within the realm of allowed possibilities, the demand for the product must exist and the product must be feasible to provide. These components are not usually easily reconciled, and a careful balancing act is required to have a product which provides sufficient protection and flexibility for the individual while remaining affordable enough to guarantee an acceptable level of income in retirement.

The role of annuity products within the pension system

Policy makers need to ensure that the rules of the pension system and limits imposed on product design facilitate the expected role of annuities in providing retirement income. The supply and demand for annuity products, and thereby the types of annuity products which are available, are influenced by the rules around how people save and spend for retirement, and thereby linked to the design of the pension system itself. The role of annuity products within the pension system is shaped by the sources of pension income in place within the system, the needs of various segments of society and any direct or indirect limits imposed on their design and function. Policy makers should therefore consider these aspects when assessing the market for annuity products and their design, in line with first guideline on global coherence comprised in the OECD Roadmap for the Good Design of DC Pension Plans.

First, annuities could be expected to play a larger role in a system with low pre-existing annuity income. Where a significant portion of an individual's retirement resources is already expected to be in annuitised form (e.g. public pension, income from a defined benefit pension), there will be less of a need for annuity products to play a large role in financing retirement. There is likely to be a much larger potential role for annuity products where a significant portion of retirement is to be funded by savings from a defined contribution plan and/or where the individual is expected to bear more of their own longevity risk.

The design of annuity products and the types of options and guarantees which are important for annuity products to provide may also depend on the structure of the pension system. For example, a high reliance on defined contribution plans may present more of a need for deferred annuities to provide investment guarantees during the accumulation phase to protect the individual against the timing risk that they will retire following a market downturn. Variable annuities, whose living benefit guarantees can provide protection against downside risk during the accumulation phase, seem to have fulfilled this need in the United States where they have increasingly gained popularity at a time when reliance on defined benefit pensions has been declining. Likewise, the potential to make withdrawals from the policy may be more important where liquidity needs can be significant in old age, for example to meet unexpected healthcare expenses.

Where policy makers see a need for annuity products to play a role in financing retirement, the rules of the pension system can be designed to make these products an explicit requirement or option. For example in Chile, savings in individual defined contribution plans is mandatory and full lump-sum payments are not allowed at retirement, except when they fall below a certain minimum income level. Individuals have the option of taking a programmed withdrawal, purchasing a life annuity, or purchasing a deferred annuity and taking programmed withdrawals temporarily until the annuity payments begin. In 2014, just over 40% of new retirees elected to purchase an annuity, though this has fallen from approximately two-thirds since the 2008 pension reform. Reasons for this could include the introduction of pension advisors to replace annuity brokers or the evolution of the implicit annuity rates compared to the allowed programmed withdrawals.

Australia is also heading in this direction and trying to make annuity products a more explicit option within their pension system following a review of the barriers to the availability of annuity products. The government is attempting to make annuities more commonly available in order to facilitate the development of deferred and variable income stream products and group-self annuitisation products (GSAs) within their mandatory funded pension system. As part of the Australian government's response to this Financial System Inquiry, the government committed to facilitating the creation of comprehensive income products for retirement (CIPRs). CIPRs would be composite products in defined contribution funds offering a balance of risk management, flexibility and higher retirement income than an account-based pension drawn down at minimum rates. They would be offered by superannuation fund trustees to their members. CIPRs would be made up of a combination of underlying products, such as an account-based pension paired with a product that provides longevity risk protection such as a deferred annuity.

While the mandatory purchase of an annuity is not common, it is effective for the development of an annuity market. For example, the United Kingdom currently has claim to the largest annuity market relative to the size of its economy, which is largely a result of the effective requirement to use a portion of the assets accumulated within a defined contribution plan to purchase a life annuity. This requirement was rescinded in 2014, which significantly reduced the demand for individual annuities. Annuity demand fell by 61% in the second quarter of 2015 compared to the second quarter of the previous year (ABI, 2015).

While mandating the purchase of annuities can be used to shape the role of annuities for retirement, any mandate for the purchase of annuity products for all segments of society would need to be done carefully to ensure that the needs of the various segments are met appropriately. The types of protection needed by consumers may vary across different tranches of society. Lower income individuals may expect a much higher proportion of their retirement to come from a public pension, and therefore may have less of a need for additional annuitised income. These individuals are also less likely to have saved a sufficient amount to purchase an annuity providing an adequate income in retirement. In 2012, for example, approximately 16% of annuities sold to pensioners in the United Kingdom were for funds of less than GBP 5 000, which would translate into a monthly income of less than 20 GBP (Financial Conduct Authority, 2014).[1] The rules for pension decumulation in Chile address this problem by stipulating that individuals can only buy an annuity if they have enough assets accumulated to get an annuity payment above a minimum level of income. Otherwise they will have to take a programmed withdrawal and the government will provide the longevity insurance when the account is exhausted. At the other end of the income spectrum, individuals may have less of a need for annuity products as they are more likely have sufficient resources to minimise the risk of outliving their savings in retirement.

Fiscal incentives can also be used by policy makers to encourage individuals to purchase annuities, either using savings from a pension savings vehicle or as a complement to existing pension savings or income. Both the Czech Republic and Estonia encourage the purchase of annuities over other payout options of pension plans by offering more favourable tax treatment for annuity payments (OECD, 2015). Regulation in the United States allows annuity products purchased outside of qualified pension savings to also function as tax-deferred savings vehicles to incentivise their purchase as a complement to other retirement income.

Differences in tax treatment have been shown to influence the decisions of pensioners to take an annuity. Lump sums in Denmark, for example, were previously taxed at a relatively advantageous flat rate for high income earners compared to annuities and programmed withdrawals. This relative advantage has since been removed and lump-sums are now declining in popularity (Rocha et al, 2011). In Korea, annuitisation of retirement savings was found to be 15 percentage points higher for savings vehicles where lump-sums are taxed compared to vehicles were lump sums are tax-free (Lee, 2016).

Nevertheless the choice of the type of annuity product by the consumer does not always align with the most beneficial tax treatment, so there may be limits to the effectiveness of such incentives. For example, in the United States traditional annuity income is tax except until the entire premium has been returned, whereas guaranteed lifetime withdrawal benefits are fully taxed as income until all interest and earnings from the contract have been withdrawn (IRI, 2011). Despite the taxation on the latter for the entire gain upfront, guaranteed withdrawal benefits have remained the most popular option for payouts from variable annuities in the United States (Geneva Association, 2013).

Beyond encouraging the take-up of annuity products, the rules governing pension accumulation and decumulation should accommodate annuity products given the potential need identified within the pension system for annuity products to provide investment and/or longevity protection. Such rules may represent indirect constraints on product design. Minimum and maximum withdrawal limits during the decumulation phase in particular may constrain the types of guarantees which can be offered by annuity products. For example, until recently, advanced life deferred annuities purchased within qualified defined contribution plans[2] in the United States did not count towards the minimum withdrawal requirement and therefore could not be used optimally to manage longevity risk. Since 2014, Qualified Longevity Annuity Contracts have now been allowed to count towards the minimum distribution requirement if the payments begin by age 85 and the annuity premium does not exceed the minimum of 25% of the account balance or USD 125 000. This allowance is expected to increase the demand for these types of deferred annuity contracts. As another example of withdrawal rules restricting the use of annuities, in the United Kingdom the allowable income from the drawdown of pension assets was previously subject to maximum and minimum levels defined by HMRC regulations. This restricted the annuity providers' ability to offer guarantees on the level of withdrawal benefit, since if the value of the fund fell below a certain threshold the guaranteed income could exceed the maximum allowed.

Policy makers should also be careful to ensure that any explicit limits with respect to market segmentation for pricing annuity products do not result in an exclusion of certain sub-groups of the population from participating in the market. Factors commonly used to rate risks for the pricing of annuity products include age, gender, health, lifestyle factors (e.g. smoking), and geographical location as these characteristics are statistically linked to the expected mortality of the individual. Using these factors for pricing allows the annuity provider to price the products appropriately for a given risk segment of the society. This limits the potential adverse selection since the price will more accurately reflect the expected longevity risk of the particular individual.

However several countries impose limitations on the personal characteristics which can be used to price the annuity product due to concerns that such segmentation could be discriminatory. For example, gender is not allowed for pricing annuity products in Europe, nor for annuity products offered within employer sponsored pension plans in the United States. Where the purchase of annuities is voluntary, such restrictions have the potential to increase adverse selection and therefore prices in the annuity markets. If males find the price of annuities too high because of their lower life expectancy and opt out of the market, prices will increase to the levels for females. This seems to have occurred in Germany, where pricing by gender has not been allowed since 2006. Annuity prices following this ban were closer to the prices charged to females prior to the new regulation (von Gaudecker and Weber, 2006). The effects of any limit on factors used for pricing should therefore be monitored.

The development of enhanced annuities in the United Kingdom has demonstrated how increased market segmentation can be beneficial for consumers, particularly where the purchase of an annuity is mandatory. Enhanced annuities offer higher payments to individuals with health conditions or risk factors which imply a lower life expectancy. Individuals eligible for these products would therefore be able to receive an annuity price which would be more 'fair' given their reduced longevity risk profile. Nevertheless these products remain uncommon outside of the United Kingdom, so perhaps more could be done to encourage their development (OECD, 2016).

Explicit limits imposed with respect to the guarantees and/or product structures which are required to be provided often aim to ensure that products are designed to meet consumers' needs. Such limits around guarantees may aim to make sure that certain risks are insured for the individual based on the market needs identified, for example by requiring indexing to inflation, as is the case in Chile and Mexico. Other limits may seek to ensure that the guarantees offered are in the consumers' best interest. In the United Kingdom, for example, the income from annuities purchased with pension savings was not allowed to decrease in absolute value, nor were certain periods of guaranteed income allowed to extend beyond 10 years. The recent reforms have allowed for more flexibility in product design, however. Other rules may require that married couples purchase a joint annuity so that the surviving beneficiary will continue to have income following the death of their spouse.

Policy makers can shape the role of annuity products through the design of the pension system considering the needs of different segments of society and ensuring the most important needs are met through any limits imposed. However, in order for these products to be used effectively, they must also be attractive to the consumer to ensure demand and be sustainable for the provider to ensure supply. Product design must therefore overcome the tension between the demands for sufficient protection, increased flexibility, and the resulting higher cost to the provider (and therefore to the consumer) of offering this.

Consumer demand: the trade-off between protection, flexibility and cost

Product design innovations have come partly as a result of traditional annuity products being unpopular and the need to compete with other investment products by offering a competitive advantage through the guarantees and flexibilities provided. Reasons often cited in the surveys received from OECD jurisdictions explaining the preference to not purchase annuities largely revolve around the inflexibility of these products and their high perceived cost. The demand for flexibility is partly driven by the reluctance of individuals to hand over their assets to an annuity provider and lock in fixed payments, giving up the potential for future increases or market participation. Consumers have expressed a desire to maintain control over their assets and investment strategies as well as fears of illiquidity. The demand for higher value products has been driven by the low perceived value of traditional products, which has only worsened in the current low interest rate environment. These trends are consistent with the trend towards increased flexibility and risk-sharing in pension plans themselves which is occurring in many jurisdictions.

Annuity providers have attempted to overcome the low levels of demand for traditional annuity products by adding product features and guarantees which address the lack of flexibility and perceived value. This has greatly increased the complexity of the menu of annuity products available on the market, which presents challenges that policy makers should be aware of. Product features aiming to increase flexibility have allowed for more participation in market returns and access to underlying funds. These types of products have demonstrated the challenges for the providers in managing the associated risks and the need for effective and robust risk management strategies. Products aiming to increase perceived value have largely incorporated more risk sharing features such as profit sharing as a way to reduce the cost of these products for the individual and the risk exposure of the annuity provider while still allowing for potential increases in future payments. These types of products highlight the need for transparency with respect to the risks shared and the underlying mechanisms involved to calculate this risk-sharing and the potential for decreases in future payments.

Annuity products available in the United States, Canada, Japan and Australia have gone more towards increasing flexibility in terms of access to the underlying capital and market participation. Retirement savings products with guaranteed income options in particular have increased the flexibility of annuity products in these markets, though these types of products have also been available to a lesser extent in Europe and the market remains small in Australia. Flexibility from these types of products is allowed for in two main ways. First, products can allow for market participation as well as various levels of control in terms of the choice of investment. Secondly, the ability to withdraw funds or even surrender the full policy can be granted.

Increased flexibility in annuity products can present a challenge for the annuity provider to manage the underlying risks and may present a trade-off in terms of cost to the consumer. For example, retirement savings products with a guaranteed income option often offer flexibility relating to market participation and investment choice. Two main risk drivers which can increase the challenge to risk management and the cost of this flexibility for these products are first, the additional optional guarantees to protect the consumer against market downturns, and secondly the uncertainty regarding the choices the consumer will make with respect to investment. These factors can increase the cost of protection, particularly where the underlying assets are invested in more volatile funds and/or funds which cannot be directly hedged by the annuity provider.

The dynamic nature of the guarantees, particularly those which tend to be offered with variable annuities, also increases the complexity of risk management strategies. This can result in additional costs relating to hedging these risks. The more flexibility offered to the consumer given these guarantees in place – for example the ability to change investment strategies – the more challenging it becomes for the annuity provider to manage the underlying risk. As a result these products do typically impose some restrictions on the decisions the consumers can take regarding the investment of their assets in order limit both risk for the annuity provider and cost for the consumer.

Flexibility in the form of the ability to withdraw from or surrender the retirement savings product with a guaranteed income option also complicates the risk management for the annuity provider offering dynamic guarantees. This is due to the increased uncertainty of the liability value at any given point in time, as the investment risks are managed and hedged based on the expected liability value taking into account assumptions regarding expected surrender. Furthermore the liability value is quite sensitive to the timing of withdrawals or surrenders and the prevailing market environment. This added uncertainty of the future value of the liability can increase the cost of providing the underlying guarantees. Surrender charges, reductions in guarantee levels and other limits are usually imposed to deter such behaviour and reduce the expected risk.

Indeed, the recent financial crisis highlighted the costs and risks of these types of guarantees, with several providers pulling out of the market. Providers then changed product designs to reduce somewhat the flexibility offered. Since then products have been significantly de-risked, reducing the levels of the guarantees and the flexibility given to the consumer with respect to investment choice as well as incorporating caps to market participation and risk-sharing features allowing consumer participation in the downside risk.

For fixed or variable payment products where the underlying assets are pooled, allowing the flexibility to withdraw or surrender funds increases the cost for consumers. This is because it diminishes one of the key benefits for consumers of traditional annuity products: the pooling of longevity risk. Traditional annuity products can offer a better payout than other comparable assets because they are able to offer an additional 'mortality premium' over the discount rate assumed due to the pooling of longevity risk for all participants. Giving the individual an opportunity to opt-out of this pooling and remove his funds could lead to a certain level of anti-selection, as those in poorer health could withdraw their funds from the pool, increasing the average life expectancy of those who remain.

The benefits of mortality pooling are less pronounced during younger ages when mortality risk is low, and therefore the option to surrender is granted more commonly during the deferral period of the annuity. Furthermore, given the very long-term nature of the contract, it may be in the consumers' best interest to retain some flexibility. Regulation in the United States dictates the extent to which annuity providers can limit the access to the underlying assets for annuitants during the accumulation phase of a deferred annuity so as to guarantee some flexibility for consumers. The Standard Non-forfeiture Law for Deferred Annuities requires and defines a minimum guaranteed value that must be provided by the annuity contract. Such value may be provided in cash through a cash surrender value, may allow for partial withdrawals, or may be provided as a guaranteed minimum paid-up value at some future retirement date.

While less common, some products do offer surrender in the payout phase, though in a limited fashion. A fixed payment annuity offered in Australia, for example, allows surrender during the first 15 years of payment, though the penalties applied if this option is exercised can be significant.

Annuity providers in European countries have tended to focus more on increasing the risk-sharing of products to reduce their cost and increase their perceived value. Profit-sharing is now quite a common feature of annuity products in Europe, though the mechanisms underlying this calculation can vary across products and/or countries. The main benefit of this feature from the annuity provider's point of view is that it is able to offer lower levels of implicit investment guarantees, paying additional payments contingent on having a surplus. The overall risk exposure for the annuity provider is thereby lower for products with profit-sharing, though in exchange the potential upside in good years is also reduced since the additional profits would be shared with policyholders. The lower cost and the potential for increasing payments in the future is attractive from the consumer's perspective. However, in exchange the individual must accept a level of uncertainty regarding the magnitude of future payments. Depending on whether a payment smoothing mechanism is used to calculate the profit-sharing, there is also a potential for significant volatility in payments. Additionally, the formula with which the additional payments are calculated is often not transparent and can be rather complex, particularly when a smoothing mechanism is imposed. This complexity necessitates transparency with respect to what risks are shared and the potential for payments to decrease in the future to ensure that the consumer understands the risk and has the capacity to absorb it.

Finding the acceptable balance in the trade-off between protection, flexibility and cost can therefore be quite challenging. Nevertheless to ensure that products are sustainable it is important to maintain this balance. Attention should be paid in particular to the balance between the protection provided to the consumer and the risks borne by the annuity provider. Allowing for increased flexibility can increase the costs for the consumer and risks for the provider, while increasing perceived value through risk-sharing results in more risk borne by the consumer. Policy makers should not necessarily prioritise one aspect over the other, but rather understand the implications with respect to the risk exposures and have the appropriate framework in place to address them. Measures must therefore be taken to make sure these risks are measured and managed going forward.

The framework and tools for managing risks to ensure the sustainability of annuity products

Increased complexity in products may also call for increased sophistication in how the potential risks of these products are identified, monitored and managed. Regulators therefore need to have a framework in place to ensure that the risks presented by annuity products for their providers are properly understood, provisioned for, and mitigated where appropriate. This framework should include having accounting and reporting standards, ensuring effective risk management strategies as well as putting in place reserve and solvency requirements which provide the incentive and ability to appropriately manage the risks that annuity products present.

Accounting standards can affect the risk exposures of an annuity provider as they influence the extent of risk-sharing for participating products and the risk management strategies for products with dynamic guarantees. First of all, accounting standards dictate how the surplus of the annuity provider is calculated and to what extent unrealised gains and losses are accounted for. For annuity products with profit-sharing features, the calculation of surplus will drive the amount that will be shared with the policyholders. Accounting rules valuing assets at historical cost will only consider realised gains and losses in the calculation of the surplus, resulting in a low volatility of the surplus calculation and a more stable basis on which to base the profit sharing calculation. Fair value accounting requiring mark-to-market valuation of assets takes unrealised gains and losses into account, thereby resulting in much more balance sheet volatility. Therefore payments to the annuitants linked to profit-sharing guarantees will also be more volatile unless a smoothing mechanism is applied. Additionally, the annuity provider may be less protected from times of low or negative profitability as it will be required to pay out a higher proportion of its assets when surpluses are positive.

Fair value accounting rules can also complicate the calculation of the share of profits to be paid to policyholders, as a portion of the unrealised gains on equity must be shared with shareholders to compensate them for the risk they bear. The formula used for the calculation of the share of profits to be paid to policyholders should be closely supervised to ensure its fairness, transparency and comparability. Germany has addressed this by stipulating a minimum participation rate for policyholders for participating annuity products. Denmark has taken another approach, providing only a guidance document for sharing profits. It has refrained from imposing strict limits on the institutions, relying on competition and transparency to ensure fairness. Each institution must, however, justify the formula and assumptions used for the calculation to the supervisor. This approach seems to have been effective in forcing institutions to consider what allocation between policyholders and shareholders is fair (Rocha, Vittas and Rudolph, 2011).

Accounting measures used to measure liabilities and earnings can also drive risk mitigation strategies. To hedge the market risk exposure from the guarantees on variable annuity contracts, for example, annuity providers must base their hedging strategy on the value of the liabilities at a given point in time. However, the liability value can differ depending on whether the GAAP, statutory or economic measure is used for valuation, and these differences can be potentially large, particularly following periods of high volatility.

The resulting effectiveness of the hedge in reducing balance sheet and earnings volatility will therefore largely depend on the accounting methodology used to report these measures. Hedging based on accounting targets other than the economic measure can result in under-hedging of certain risks such as interest rates. To the extent that regulation relies more on GAAP or statutory measures for assessing the financial health of the annuity provider, there may be less incentive for the annuity provider to hedge its liabilities on an economic basis, leaving it exposed to more risk.

Hedge accounting in the United States helps to limit the volatility of financial reporting. According to SSAP No. 86, derivative instruments used in effective hedges are valued and reported in a manner consistent with the hedged asset or liability. For instance, if a position qualifies as hedging effective and the instrument being hedged is reported at amortised cost, then the hedging instrument would also be reported at amortised cost. Derivative instruments used in hedging transactions that are not deemed hedge-effective are reported at fair value, and changes in fair value are recorded as unrealised gains or losses.

Reporting requirements can help supervisors to monitor the amount of risk being taken on by the annuity provider and the effectiveness of the risk management strategies implemented. Investment in derivatives in particular has become a focus of supervisors in light of their use by annuity providers to hedge their market risk exposure. Supervisors therefore have an interest in monitoring the overall exposure of annuity providers to financial derivatives as well as ensuring that their use for hedging risk exposures is appropriate and effective.

Clear and transparent reporting standard with respect to derivatives allow for a better monitoring of derivative exposure and their relative significance in terms of overall investment. Annuity providers in the United States report derivative investment by purpose, type of derivative, type of contract and industry segment, which allows for the identification of trends in derivative investment strategies over time. At the end of 2014, derivative investment represented just under 1% of total insurance assets, but has grown rapidly. The notional value of derivative investment that was being used for hedging strategies was 94% of total derivative investment by insurers, with 65% of this used for hedging interest rate risk and 23% for hedging equity risk (NAIC, 2015).

The use of derivatives by annuity providers to hedge their risks should also be monitored for effectiveness. The financial crisis made clear the benefits of hedging market risk with derivative instruments, but also revealed its shortcomings and limitations. Variable annuity providers who were not sufficiently hedging the guarantees they were offering were forced to exit the market following significant losses from the combination of the drop in equity markets, increased volatility and low interest rates. However even those providers who were actively hedging their risks experienced significant losses due to the approximate nature of the dynamic hedging strategies implemented, although these strategies did save them billions more in losses.

Two key lessons can be drawn from the crisis in terms of the potential effectiveness of risk management strategies which supervisors should be aware of. First is the potential significance of basis risk, the difference between the changes in the index used to hedge and the change in the underlying investment, and secondly is the importance of assumptions around the behaviour of customers, in particular with respect to withdrawal and surrender behaviour. In response to the former, in addition to reducing the generosity of the guarantees provided, annuity providers have also moved to limit the investment options available to the consumer to those which would be exposed to less basis risk when hedged with exchange traded options. Secondly, behavioural assumptions have been revised to be more in line with observed experience. Given the unpredictability of this latter risk, however, customer behaviour remains a variable to be closely monitored and the dynamic nature of the risk better understood through sensitivity exercises and scenario testing.

Therefore, while derivatives have proven to be very valuable as risk management tools for annuity providers and should be allowed to be used as such, regulators have an interest in ensuring that their use is effective and does not increase overall risk exposure. The effectiveness of hedging strategies in offsetting risk exposure should be tracked and reported to monitor the efficacy of the derivative transactions for risk management purposes. With this aim, several countries, including Canada and the United States, require that annuity providers submit a clearly stated strategy to the regulators detailing their planned use of derivatives for their risk management and the objectives to be achieved. Similarly, other countries such as Japan require that the terms of each derivative transaction and its purpose be identifiable. The United Kingdom does not allow derivatives which are not used for the purpose of hedging to be recognised as a capital resource for the insurer.

Given the added exposure to counterparty credit risk with the use of OTC derivatives, however, regulatory measures should be put in place to ensure that this risk is mitigated and that these instruments are effective in reducing overall risk exposure. Jurisdictions have addressed this issue in various ways. Counterparties can be required to meet certain standards, for example a certain credit rating as in Chile. Concentration limits to counterparty exposure may also be put in place. Recent regulations such as the Dodd-Frank Act in the United States and the European Market Infrastructure Regulation (EMIR) in Europe have sought to reduce counterparty risk through increased transparency and collateralisation requirements. Standardised OTC derivatives are increasingly being required to be cleared through central counterparties who are subject to strict collateral requirements and have risk neutral objectives. Collateral is also generally required to be posted for bilateral OTC transactions.

Additional requirements imposed to mitigate counterparty risk should nevertheless be effective in reducing overall risk exposure. Increased liquidity risk to meet margin calls could pose a challenge for annuity providers given the long term nature of their guarantees and investment horizon. Regulators should ensure that the additional costs from stricter collateral requirements are not so burdensome as to reduce the incentives of annuity providers to hedge their risks. In Australia, life insurers are permitted to create a charge over fund assets to meet margin requirements for exchange traded derivatives, though this is not currently allowed for over-the-counter derivatives.

Reserve and solvency requirements for annuity products need to keep up with the evolving complexity of the products to ensure that all guarantees are appropriately provisioned for. Reserve requirements generally rely on the valuation of annuity liabilities using assumptions which include a certain level of margin and are historically based on rather prescriptive formulas. The formulaic approach is now beginning to change with the movement towards principles-based requirements in an effort to better represent increasingly complex products and guarantees.[3] As such, reserve requirements have typically responded to the evolution in product design rather than the other way around.

As an example of the traditional formulaic approach, reserve requirements in the United States under statutory accounting for fixed annuities are based on the Commissioners Annuity Reserve Valuation Method (CARVM). Reserves for deferred annuities reflect the greatest present value of guaranteed benefits, do not account for mortality probabilities during deferral, and assume all options are exercised by the policyholder in their best interest (Sharp, 1999). The valuation rate and mortality table are defined by regulation and vary depending on product type and date of issue (Model Regulation Service, 2012). In addition, the Standard Valuation Law requires that the minimum reserve for deferred annuities be tested for adequacy by conducting an asset adequacy analysis based on cash flow testing of the assets and liabilities under a variety of interest rate scenarios.

Canada is slightly more flexible in its approach, and annuity reserves follow the Policy Premium Method (PPM) and are based on the present value of expected future cash flows valued using best estimate assumptions with an appropriate margin. Expected future cash flows account for both the probability of death and the probability of surrender, where applicable. Margins are set following guidance offered by the Canadian Institute of Actuaries (CIA), with the level of conservatism depending on considerations such as the type of product and investment policy (e.g. dividend payments and duration matching). Cash flows must be discounted under several economic scenarios, and the reserve set appropriately to capture most of the range of results. Reinsurance can be reflected (Society of Actuaries, 1997).

Australia takes a similar approach to Canada for reserving requirements for life annuities, which are based on best estimate assumptions plus a margin to allow for a uniform emergence of profit. The discount rate used must be the risk-free rate unless the benefits are contractually linked to the performance of the underlying assets.

However, formulaic requirements which rely on static factors cannot accurately capture the liability value where dynamic guarantees are involved. With the increased complexity presented by variable annuities for example, the reserve requirement for these products in the United States has evolved to a more principles-based approach which relies on valuation using stochastic market scenarios, with reserves set at the conditional tail expectation at the 70% level of confidence (CTE 70), which is the average of the worst 30% of the scenarios.[4]

Similar to the requirements in the United States for variable annuities, the CIA has published guidance for the valuation of variable annuities, (known as segregated funds), which should be calculated based on stochastic modelling to calculate the guaranteed minimum benefits owed net of the account value. The confidence level should be set between 60% and 80% CTE. (CIA, 2010).

The Financial Services Agency (FSA) responded in Japan to the complexity of variable annuity products by requiring a valuation of all guarantees based on risk-neutral scenarios assuming no lapse and full utilisation of guarantees, as well as requiring an accumulation of additional contingency reserves to cover an unfavourable market condition occurring once in every ten years. In addition, the FSA requires firms to accumulate the risk capital corresponding to the additional guaranteed minimum to cover an unfavourable market condition occurring once every two decades. Thus the FSA has developed regulation and supervision which guides insurers to conduct proper risk management by requiring the accumulation of contingency reserves and regulating the solvency margin.

In the United Kingdom, reserve requirements evolved for the with-profits business to better reflect the value of any embedded options and guarantees in the reserves. Reserves for these products must be the maximum of 1) the mathematical reserve based on prudent assumptions and gross premiums and 2) a realistic calculation based on best estimate assumptions which explicitly takes into account expected discretionary bonus payments. Reinsurance may be accounted for so long as there is an effective transfer of risk.

There is therefore a clear movement towards more flexible and principles-based reserving requirements to better account for the risks in increasingly complex products. Additionally, the movement away from strict formulaic requirements may also help to align the incentives of the annuity providers with the economic reality. The prescription of reserve formulas which do not always align with the actuarial liability value could leave room for regulatory arbitrage and perverse incentives for the management of insurance companies. For example, at the onset of the financial crisis in 2008 and 2009, there is some evidence that some insurance companies in the United States were offering deeply discounted prices for annuities because the reserve formula implied a requirement below the actuarial value of the annuity and the additional sales boosted the balance sheet (Koijen and Yogo, 2013). On the other hand, alignment can also pose challenges, as experienced in Australia where the reserve requirements can lead to a provisioning strain if the investment yield offered to customers exceeds the risk-free rate used in valuing the liabilities.

It is also important that reserve and solvency requirements reflect reduced risk from any risk mitigation that the annuity provider has undertaken. This can incentivise the annuity provider to reduce its risk exposures where appropriate in order to reduce its reserving and capital requirements. Both Canada and the United States, for example, recognise hedging of the market risk from variable annuities for reserving and solvency calculations. In the United States, however, hedging can only be reflected if the insurer has a Clearly Defined Hedging Strategy in place, and hedge effectiveness assumed cannot exceed 70% (Covington, 2012).

As with reserves, solvency requirements for insurers have historically been prescribed and formulaic but are moving towards more flexible and principles-based approaches as increasingly complex products are introduced to the market. Solvency requirements are additional capital requirements on top of reserves which insurers are required to have available in order to be able to sustain adverse shocks to the business. Reserve calculations usually already include significant margins on the assumptions used for their calculation for the purpose of covering adverse deviations. These margins usually also count towards the solvency capital requirements. Therefore, the calculation of the solvency requirement can be viewed as the capital requirement including the margins embedded in the reserves.

The United States and Canada were among the first countries to impose risk-based solvency requirements, with both regimes defining factors to be applied to balance sheet items to calculate the required capital. As a response to the development of guarantees on annuity products which are highly sensitive to interest rate movements, the required capital for interest rate risk in the United States is now based on stochastic scenarios and calculated at the 90% CTE. Canada has retained a rather complex formula for these types of products, though the use of internal models with stochastic modelling is allowed, with the recommended security level of 95% CTE to be consistent with the security level on which the standard factors are based. Hedging is allowed to be taken into account, though the maximum hedging effectiveness which can be assumed is 95% and 50% for the United States and Canada, respectively.

The United Kingdom requires additional stress and scenario testing to ensure the insurer's ability to meet its liabilities under a wide range of situations relevant to its particular risk profile in addition to the minimum capital requirement calculated using risk-based factors.

The new Solvency II regime in Europe moves away from the formulaic approach of Solvency I, and aims to align solvency capital requirements across Europe and make them more sensitive to the risk exposure of insurers. The new requirements are based on market consistent valuation (mark-to-market for assets and mark-to-model for liabilities) at a security level of 99.5% Value at Risk (VaR).

Similarly, the Australia Prudential Regulation Authority (APRA) recently overhauled the framework for insurer solvency capital requirements with the objectives to improve the risk-sensitivity of the capital requirements and to better align them with international standards. The new Life and General Insurance Capital (LAGIC) standards became effective on January 1, 2013. Risk charges are set to ensure a 99.5% probability of capital adequacy over a one year time horizon (APRA, 2012).

There are some concerns that a market-consistent approach will restrict the ability of insurance companies to offer long-term guarantees by increasing pro-cyclicality and the ability to recognise expected returns above the risk-free rate. Various counter-cyclical mechanisms have been considered and/or implemented to address this issue. For example, Solvency II allows for a matching adjustment which would reflect an illiquidity premium in the discount rate for liabilities. Australia allows for discounting the liabilities based on the risk-free rate plus an illiquidity premium determined using a prescribed formula based on the published spread between A-rated corporate and Commonwealth Government bond yields.

The movement towards principles-based approaches for reserves and solvency has also resulted in an increased allowance for internal models to better reflect the individual risk profiles of insurers. Solvency II in Europe and LAGIC in Australia, for example, both allow for the use of internal models for calculating capital requirements. Nevertheless, this is not the case in all jurisdictions. In the United States, regulators are reluctant to allow the use of full internal models due to higher costs and reduced comparability and transparency (SMI Task Force, 2013). Another potential motivation for this is the legal standards in the United States. An approach which remains objective and formulaic could be less subject to legal challenge (Bahna-Nolan et al, 2013).

The allowance for an internal model for calculating reserve and/or solvency requirements presents both advantages and disadvantages from a supervisory perspective. On one hand, allowing for an internal model gives the annuity provider the opportunity to better adapt the model to reflect the risk profile of its products and business, and may capture certain risk dynamics that a standard model would miss. On the other hand, implementing internal models are more costly and resource intensive and can lead to reduced transparency and comparability across companies. These pros and cons must be weighed in the decision of whether to maintain an objective standard model for these calculations or to allow annuity providers to develop their own models. Any internal model should be subject to careful regulatory review and approval to ensure that assumptions used are appropriate and that all relevant risks are captured.

The evolution in annuity product design necessitates a framework which recognises and accounts for the risks presented and the risk management strategies employed in order to ensure that these products are sustainable for the long term. Policy makers need to understand how accounting standards can affect the measurement of risk and the resulting incentives to manage this risk. Reporting standards can aid in the monitoring of the effectiveness of risk management strategies, particularly with respect to the use of derivative instruments to hedge market risk exposure. Finally, reserve and solvency requirements that are more principles-based rather than formulaic are better able to adapt to innovations in annuity product design and therefore more fully reflect the resulting risks that these products present.

With this framework in place, regulators then need to also ensure that annuity products are transparent and understood by the consumer. These issues relating to consumer protection will be the focus of the following chapter.

Notes

1. Based on the estimation that 60% of annuitants get an annuity from their existing provider, and 27% of these have pension pots under 5000 GBP. The FCA indicates that for premiums less than 5 000 the rates are around 4.25%, and the rates are around 5.1% for premiums between 5 000 and 10 000.
2. 401(a), a 403(b) plan, a governmental 457(b) plan or a traditional IRA.
3. The term complex products is used in a descriptive manner and does not refer to any legal definition of complex products.
4. The Conditional Tail Expectation (CTE) at a given confidence level is defined as the average of all outcomes beyond the confidence level. Therefore the CTE 70 would be the average of all outcomes beyond the 70th percentile, or the average of the worst 30% of scenarios. The CTE is alternatively known as the Tail-VaR or the Conditional Value at Risk (CVaR).

References

ABI (2015), "UK Insurance & Long Term Savings Key Facts 2015".

APRA (2012), "Life and General Insurance Capital Review October 2012", *Prudential Standards – October 2012, Life Insurance, www.apra.gov.au/CrossIndustry/Pages/Life-and-General-Insurance-Capital-Review-October-2012.aspx.*

Bahna-Nolan, M. et al (2013), "Life Insurance Regulatory Structures and Strategy: EU compared with US", for the Committee on Finance Research and CAS, CIA, SOA Joint Risk Management Section, Casualty Actuarial Society, Canadian Institute of Actuaries, Society of Actuaries.

CIA (2010), "Report of the Task Force on Segregated Fund Liability and Capital Methodologies", *Document 210053*, Canadian Institute of Actuaries, Ottawa.

Covington, L. (2012), "U.S. Annuity Market Dynamics and Regulatory Requirements", *OECD Roundtable on Annuities, http://irionline.org/docs/default-source/default-document-library/oecd-presentation.pdf?sfvrsn=0.*

Financial Conduct Authority (2015), "Retirement income market study: Final report – confirmed findings and remedies".

Financial Conduct Authority (2014), "Thematic Review of Annuities".

Geneva Association (2013), "Variable Annuities – An analysis of Financial Stability", The Geneva Association, Geneva.

The Investment Research Institute (2011), "The Tax Advantage of Annuities: How Tax Deferral and Guaranteed Lifetime Strategies Can Benefit All Consumers".

Koijen, R., M. Yogo (2013), "The Cost of Financial Frictions for Life Insurers".

Lee, K. (2016), "Analysis of payout choice from individual deferred annuities in Korea", *Journal of Pension Economics & Finance*, Vol 15/2, pp. 224-248.

Model Regulation Service (2013), "Standard Valuation Law", National Association of Insurance Commissioners.

National Association of Insurance Commissioners (NAIC) (2015), "Update on the Insurance Industry's Use of Derivatives and Exposure Trends", *Capital Markets Special Report, http://www.naic.org/capital_markets_archive/150807.htm*

OECD (2016), Chapter 6: "Fragmentation of retirement markets due to differences in life expectancy", in *OECD Business and Finance Outlook 2016*, OECD Publishing, Paris. *http://dx.doi.org/10.1787/9789264257573-en*

OECD (2015), "The tax treatment of funded private pension plans in OECD and EU countries", *www.oecd.org/tax/tax-treatment-funded-private-pension-plans-oecd-eu-countries.htm*

Rocha, R., D. Vittas, H. P. Rudolph (2011), "Annuities and Other Retirement Products: Designing the Payout Phase", World Bank, Washington D.C.

Sharp, K. P. (1999), "Commissioners Annuity Reserve Valuation Method", *Journal of Actuarial Practice*, Vol. 7

Society of Actuaries (1997), "A Comparison of Canadian and U.S. Reserving Methods and their Financial Implications", *Montreal Spring Meeting, Record Volume 23 No. 2*, Society of Actuaries.

Solvency Modernization Initiative Task Force (2013), "The U.S. National State-based System of Insurance Financial Regulation and the Solvency Modernization Initiative", *NAIC White Paper*, National Association of Insurance Commissioners.

von Gaudecker, H.-M., & Weber, C. (2004). "Surprises in a Growing Market Niche: An Evaluation of the German Private Life Annuities Market", *The Geneva Papers on Risk and Insurance*, 29(3), 394-416.

Chapter 5

Ensuring suitable products for consumers*

This chapter discusses what can be done by policy makers to help ensure that consumers get annuity products which are suitable for their needs and to ensure that appropriate consumer protections are in place. The increasing complexity and risk-sharing presented by different annuity products brings many challenges with respect to making sure that consumers are aware of the products available, can access the best product for their needs, and understand the products they are purchasing and the costs and risks that they entail. Policy makers must ensure that information is readily available and used by consumers, that products are clearly presented in a comprehensible and unbiased manner, and that product disclosures are transparent with respect to the product's features, costs and risks and in order to help consumers choose the most suitable product for their needs.

* This chapter draws upon and reflects in part the 2011 G20/OECD High-Level Principles on Financial Consumer Protection (G20/OECD, 2011) and the Effective Approaches to Support their Implementation (G20/OECD 2013, 2014) endorsed by the G20 in 2013 and 2014. The High-Level Principles are of interest across all financial services sectors – including, banking and credit, investment, securities and insurance and pensions and are designed to assist interested jurisdictions to enhance financial consumer protection. The principles complement and do not substitute any existing international principles and/or guidelines and they do not address sector specific issues. However, the principles are supporting and inter-connected, thereby reflecting a holistic but proportionate approach to financial consumer protection.

Product awareness

Product awareness can lead to better outcomes for consumers not only by providing consumers the opportunity to choose, but also by eventually leading to better value products. However, the latter outcome is not a given, and requires consumers to act upon the product information they receive. Consumers first need to know what annuity options are available to them in order to have the opportunity to select a product which will meet their needs and best interests.[1] If this increased product awareness then also leads consumers to more actively compare prices of different products, this could also create more pressure for annuity providers to offer competitive quotes, leading to better value products for consumers.[2]

This issue is particularly important where annuities are expected to play an integral role in providing retirement income. Two markets provide examples where this has been the case: the United Kingdom where the annuitisation of DC pension assets was effectively mandatory, and in Chile where consumers must decide between a programmed withdrawal and an annuity at retirement. These markets both provide interesting and relevant examples to demonstrate the challenges and solutions for policy makers to not only try to make information available, but also to get consumers to actively use the information and compare products to select the most suitable one.

A lack of awareness with respect to available products can lead individuals to get a less suitable annuity product than they otherwise should have. Following the observation that most individuals purchased an annuity product from their existing pension provider and failed to look for other options available on the open market, regulators in the United Kingdom required pension providers to inform their clients of their right to shop around and change providers. While these rules were effective in increasing awareness of the possibility of shopping around, a third of the individuals still failed to do so and therefore remained unaware of the other products and offers available to them. Furthermore, despite the fact that two-thirds of individuals did shop around, 60% still purchased an annuity with their existing provider in 2012. The Financial Conduct Authority estimated that 80% of these individuals could have gotten a better deal elsewhere and that half of them could have increased their income by at least 5% (Financial Conduct Authority, 2014).

The problem of consumers not getting the best deal was driven not only by consumers failing to shop around for a better price, but also from their lack of awareness of the existence of enhanced annuities. Enhanced annuities pay a higher income to individuals with health problems or lifestyle factors which decrease their life expectancy. Individuals eligible to purchase an enhanced annuity but not aware of this option therefore received significantly lower income than they otherwise could have.

The underlying driver of this unwillingness to actively search out the best available annuity option seems to be the inertia of individuals to go with the flow and stick with the 'default' or easiest option. This tendency poses a particular problem when the decision being faced is complex, which is certainly the case when deciding what annuity to buy as the individual has to evaluate numerous uncertain variables including how long they will live and future inflation. The individual faces the choice of simply taking the offer from their existing provider, or spending considerable amounts of cognitive effort and time in searching for a better option. The 'wake-up pack' required to be sent to them to inform them of their options for retirement was also found to be too long and complex for many, resulting in a disengagement from the process of transitioning into retirement. Furthermore customers may feel that they have built up a relationship with their existing provider and trust the offer provided. The tendency to take the initial annuity offer is therefore quite persistent and prevalent (Financial Conduct Authority, 2014; 2015).

This is a particular problem especially given that there is some evidence that some pension providers were taking advantage of this tendency by not providing their existing customers a competitive offer. In some cases, the price being offered on the open market for the equivalent product was better than that being charged to an existing customer. In other cases, individuals were not offered or informed about the option of purchasing an enhanced annuity even if they were eligible for one (Financial Conduct Authority, 2014).

In response to these observations, the Financial Conduct Authority is proposing several remedies to try to further engage consumers in the process of selecting an annuity and incite them to shop around and to ultimately improve the competitiveness of the market. First, the wake-up pack will be redesigned to be easier to comprehend. Several designs will be tested with annuity providers and consumers to determine the most effective method of communication and presentation of options in order to maximize consumer engagement and comprehension. Secondly, firms will be required to provide information about how their annuity quote compares with quotes found on the open market and to highlight the differences in resulting income. This could both help to incite firms to offer more competitive rates as well as make the benefits of shopping around more salient to the consumer. Finally, firms are required to direct their consumers to seek guidance from the free, government provided service Pension Wise (Financial Conduct Authority, 2015).

Chile takes an alternative approach to ensuring that consumers are aware of their options by centralising the source of this information and requiring a choice to be made among the various options. Once individuals have indicated that they plan to retire, the pension fund transmits their information to an electronic platform, the SCOMP, which then provides consumers comparable information regarding their options to take a programmed withdrawal from a pension fund or take a life annuity from an insurance company (Stanko and Paklina, 2014). The individual is therefore forced to choose an option, making them much less prone to the effects of inertia and staying with their current pension provider, and encouraging them to actively consider the option to purchase an annuity. Indeed, in 2015 approximately 50% of pensioners had life annuities provided by an insurance company (Superintendencia de Pensiones, 2015).

Chile's approach with the SCOMP has also succeeded in nurturing a very competitive market for annuity products in Chile. Forcing consumers to actively compare prices and select an option increases the competitive pressure on annuity providers to offer better rates. Partly as a result of this system, Chile has one of the highest money's worth ratios for annuities of any annuity market, implying that consumers are getting very good value for their premiums. Money's worth ratios are a direct measure of the value the annuity product offers and thereby can provide an indication of the extent to which annuity rates offered are competitive. However, supervisors do need to ensure that these ratios are not unsustainably high, resulting in excessive investment risk-taking by the annuity provider or unprofitable products.

Box 5.1 explains the money's worth ratio and provides some international comparisons of the ratios for different annuity markets.

Box 5.1. **Money's worth ratios**

The money's worth ratio (MWR) is a measure commonly used to demonstrate the value of annuity products being offered in the market with respect to their actual cost. It essentially represents the ratio of the actuarially fair premium of the annuity – or the present expected value of the future annuity cash flows – over the actual market price of the annuity. A ratio of 1 would mean that the price of an annuity is exactly its actuarial fair value. In practice we would expect a ratio of less than one, as the annuity provider would normally need to include a margin to cover its expenses and the risk of an adverse deviation in the assumptions used to price the annuity, for example due to higher than expected mortality improvements.

The mortality rates and discount rates assumed to calculate the actuarial fair premium are significant drivers of the resulting MWR. Changing these underlying assumptions will change the numerator of the MWR and thereby impact the resulting ratio. The denominator of this ratio remains constant as it represents the actual observed market price of the annuity.

The mortality rates assumed for the actuarially fair annuity value can be based on the general population or on the annuitant population. The annuitant population usually experiences lower mortality and therefore has a higher life expectancy than that of the general population. This is primarily due to the anti-selection in the annuity market; individuals having a higher life expectancy also tend to be more likely to purchase a life annuity. The magnitude of this difference varies by country and is also dependent on the structure of the pension system itself. For example, higher anti-selection can be expected where the purchase of an annuity is voluntary, resulting in a larger difference between annuitant mortality and that of the general population.

An actuarially fair annuity value calculated on the basis of the annuitant mortality will therefore be higher than the value assuming mortality of the general population. This reflects the expectation that payments will be made for a longer period of time given the higher life expectancy of the annuitant population.

Annuity providers take this expected difference in mortality into account by basing the price of the products on the annuitant mortality. Therefore the observed price of the annuity product would be expected to be closer to the actuarially fair annuity value also based on annuitant mortality, and would represent a lower value to an average individual in the population who can expect to live to a lower age compared to an average annuitant.

As a result, the MWR will also be lower when the actuarially fair premium (the numerator) is based on the mortality of the general population. This is observed in the MWRs calculated for the US in 1998 (see Table 5.1), which increase by 10 percentage points when the ratio is based on the annuitant mortality.

Discount rates used for the calculation of the actuarially fair premium can be based on the risk-free rates (government bonds, swaps) or on the term structure of higher yielding instruments such as corporate bonds. The annuity value based on lower risk free rates will be higher than one based on a higher discount rate. Risk-free rates are generally assumed for these calculations, however, as annuities are seen to be riskless or very low-risk investments, similar to an investment in government bonds.

The MWR based on a risk-free rate will be higher than one based on corporate bond yields. This difference can be significant, as demonstrated in Canada where the MWR based on risk-free rates is 15 percentage points higher than the ratio based on corporate bond yields.

However, the MWR calculated in several markets based on risk-free rates has turned out to be near or even higher than 1, for example in Chile and Canada, which would be an unsustainable situation for the annuity provider investing in the low yielding risk-free government bonds. The primary explanation given for this observation is that annuity providers must be investing in higher yielding and risker assets in order to sustain their profitability, allowing them to be able to offer annuities which provide a comparable return to other risk-free investments. This results in a higher value of the annuity products for individuals.

Table 5.1. **Money's worth ratios for selected annuity markets**

Country	Annuity type	Mortality	Discount	Period	MWR	Comments
Chile[a]	Single life, real	Annuitant	Risk-free	Avg. 2005-2008	109%	Increasing
Canada[b]	Single life, 65, level	Annuitant	Risk-free	Avg. 2000-2009	100-105%	Fairly stable, spiked during crisis
Canada	Single life, 65, level	Annuitant	Corporate Bond	Avg. 2000-2009	85-90%	
Germany[c]	Participating life, 65, male	Annuitant	Risk-free	2003	98%	Takes participation into account
Netherlands[d]	Single life, 65	Pensioner	Swaps	2010, 2012	104%, 95%	Increasing through 2005-2009, then decreasing
Singapore[e]	Single life, 65, male	Annuitant	Risk-free	2007	95%	
UK[f]	Single life, 65, male, voluntary	Annuitant	Risk-free	Avg. 2005-2009	86%	Has fallen from 95/100% over last decade
UK	Single life, 65, level, male, compulsory	Pensioner Lives	Risk-free	2009	85-90%	
UK	Single life, 65, real male, compulsory	Pensioner Lives	Risk-free	2009	72%-80%	
UK	Single life, 65, level, male, compulsory	Retirement Annuity Contracts	Risk-free	2007	95%	
US[g]	Single life, 65, nominal	Population	Risk-free	1998	87%	
US	Single life, 65, nominal	Annuitant	Risk-free	1998	97%	
US	Single life, 65, real	Population	Risk-free	1998	70%	
US	Single life, 65, real	Annuitant	Risk-free	1998	80%	

a. (Mitchell & Ruiz, 2009)
b. (Milevsky & Shao, 2010)
c. (von Gaudecker & Weber, Surprises in a Growing Market Niche: An Evaluation of the German Private Life Annuities Market, 2004)
d. (Cannon, Stevens, & Tonks, 2013)
e. (Fong, Lemaire, & Tse, 2011)
f. (Cannon & Tonks, 2010)
g. (Mitchell, et al., 1999)

The complexity of the decision of how to finance one's retirement leads many consumers to disengage from the process and go with the option which requires the least effort rather than spending the time and cognitive effort to inform themselves of all their options. To the extent that this does not lead to the best outcomes for individuals, policy makers will need to intervene as this is not a problem which will easily resolve itself in the market. Forcing consumers to consider the alternative options and make a choice seems to be effective at increasing their engagement in the decision and encouraging providers to offer competitive rates, resulting in better value for the consumer.

Product distribution

Once consumers are aware of their options, they will then need to go through a distribution channel to have access to the annuity products. The increased complexity of products also implies an increased need for reliance on financial advice. This advice can significantly influence consumers' decisions, therefore policy makers need to make sure that this advice is appropriate and does not lead consumers to select a product which is not optimal for them.

Ensuring that financial advice relating to annuity products is unbiased and in the interests of the client is particularly important for annuity products, as the decision to take an annuity product is often either irreversible or quite costly to reverse. However, the potential conflicts of interest that the financial intermediary may face can present a challenge to ensuring that advice is objective and unbiased. These conflicts primarily arise in the way that these advisors are compensated for their services. For annuity products, as with other insurance products, compensation is often in the form of a commission paid to the distributor upon the completion of a transaction. This could create incentives for the advisor to recommend the annuity product paying the highest commission rather than the one that is most suitable for the client. Much evidence indicates that the advice of financial intermediaries is indeed influenced by the commissions they receive (e.g. Christoffersen et al., 2012; Hackethal et al., 2012; Mullainathan et al., 2011). An example relating to annuities in particular is found in Chile, where only around 20% of the individuals receiving advice from a tied insurance agent – whose commission is dependent on the sale of the annuity product from the insurance company that they represent – selected the best annuity quote offered, compared to around 60% of individuals soliciting advice from an independent pension advisor (Stanko and Paklina, 2014).

Regulation addressing this issue largely aims to ensure that the intermediaries for these distribution channels are competent and have the consumers' interests in mind.[3] The types of regulation imposed can include duty of care requirements, disclosure of commission payments, restrictions on the distributor's compensation structure, standards for the intermediaries and products offered and/or giving consumers the opportunity to change their minds.[4]

Duty of care standards impose an ethical duty on the intermediary to provide advice which is in the interests of the client. Fiduciary duty (or equivalent) requirements define a legal relationship where the intermediary must act in the best interest of the consumer. This is typically applied to financial advisors but can also apply to employers providing pension plans, for example, where the employer is bound to manage the plan in the interests of their employees. For employers offering defined contribution plans, this obligation can extend to the investment options which are offered within the plan.

This legal duty has been identified as one reason that annuity products are rarely offered as an option within employer sponsored pension plans in the United States, as the employer could face legal action if the annuity provider fails to provide future payments. In attempt to reduce employers' reluctance to make annuity products available, the US Department of Labor has tried to clarify the duties of the employer to continuously monitor the annuity provider's health and has defined a statute of limitations after which legal action cannot be taken against the employer. Some Canadian DC plan administrators have also been concerned about the fiduciary duty under pension legislation as it applies in relation to providing information and advice on annuities. The concern was around the extent that they could be held liable if a former plan member experiences problems with a retirement product about which they received information or advice from the plan administrator. Canadian pension regulators have therefore proposed guidelines for providing standardised information about annuities.

The responsibilities of plan sponsors or administrators in performing due-diligence in their selection of annuity products to fulfil any fiduciary obligations need to be extremely clear in order to avoid ambiguities which could lead to a reluctance for plan sponsors to make annuity products available. Standardising how information about annuity products is provided to the members could also help them to be sure that they have fulfilled their obligations in providing information to their members regarding the options available and that their fiduciary duty has not been breached.

The extent to which retail distributors are subject to fiduciary duty may depend on the type of services they provide and the particular products they offer. For example, in the United States the definition of a fiduciary for financial advice for retirement was until recently quite narrow, requiring specific and personalised recommendations to be provided on an ongoing basis in order to be subject to fiduciary duties defined under the Employee Retirement Income Security Act (ERISA). However, the Conflicts of Interest rule passed in April 2016 expanded the application of fiduciary best interest standards to all advisors providing investment advice for retirement plans. Registered investment advisors in the United States are also subject to a fiduciary standard of care which, in general terms, requires that the adviser take into account a number of considerations, such as whether the fees are reasonable, whether the investments are adequately diversified, whether there are conflicts of interest, and whether the investments are consistent with the provisions of the trust or other governing documents. However, broker dealers, insurance salespersons or any other financial company representative not subject to a fiduciary standard operate under a suitability standard, which only requires a determination that an investment is suitable for the client. This standard is much less stringent and difficult to legally challenge if the consumer ends up with a product which was not fully appropriate for them.

Disclosure of commissions is commonly required as a way to prevent biased advice and ensure that individuals are aware of any potential conflicts of interest that their financial advisor may have, however disclosure alone has often been shown to be ineffective (e.g. Hung et al., 2015; Oxera, 2014). The United Kingdom tried several approaches which seemed to have made no difference in the uptake of conflicted advice. Standard disclosures were found to be ineffective as most of the time individuals did not even engage with the disclosure. A menu of commissions was then required, which was essentially a price list for the various services provided which also included information on the market average price. This also had little impact as advisers did not clearly communicate the information and individuals tended to trust their own financial advisor.

Another risk with the disclosure of commission payments is that consumers may place excessive weight on this information when making a purchase decision, which could overshadow the overall product's appropriateness and value, particularly where several different fees are disclosed. A study by the US Federal Trade Commission showed that consumers focused too much on the commission information for mortgage brokers and ended up paying more than they otherwise would have (Federal Trade Commission, 2004). While disclosure could and should be part of the solution to address conflicts of interest, it seems that these requirements need to be structured carefully and are alone not sufficient to solve the problem.

Different approaches have been taken across jurisdictions with respect to the allowable compensation structure to try to better align the interests of the consumer and advisor. For example, commissions can be contingent on the longevity of the purchase. Germany requires that the distribution costs be spread over the first five years of the contract, and part of these costs must be repaid if the product is terminated early. Chile has put in place a cap of 2% on the intermediation fee which could be charged to consumers purchasing an annuity in response to a steady increase of these fees which had been observed, reaching highs of nearly 6% in 2000. Fees subsequently came down resulting in a better value of the annuity product for the consumer (Stanko and Paklina, 2014). Other countries such as Australia, Denmark, the Netherlands and the United Kingdom have gone farther by banning commissions completely for certain intermediaries, allowing only fee-based advice services to be provided. While this ban does not currently affect non-advised annuity sales in the United Kingdom, the FCA is considering banning commissions for these products as well (Financial Conduct Authority, 2015).

Nevertheless, concerns have been raised that banning commissions completely could reduce the availability and take-up of financial advice. First, advisers may leave or be forced out of the market as a result of a ban on commissions. Indeed, the United Kingdom has observed a downward trend in the number of advisers, which fell to 24 000 in 2014 from 26 000 in 2011, though this may also be due in part to changes in qualification standards (Financial Conduct Authority, 2015). Secondly, while individuals have always been paying for advice through commissions, making this cost more transparent might deter them from seeking advice at all or make advice less available for individuals with smaller pension savings. The United Kingdom has observed a drop observed in the provision of financial advice, with more consumers making purchase decisions on their own, even though non-advised products are still allowed to pay commissions (Financial Conduct Authority, 2015). In Germany also, where the consumer has the choice between commissions-based or fee-based advice, demand for the fee-based advice remains limited and consumers seem to favour fees paid through commissions.

Regulation and supervision of the products themselves have also been used to address potential problems of misselling or market inefficiencies. The Netherlands has introduced additional product oversight rules to ensure the quality and appropriateness of products following the observation that some of the products sold were so complex that even advisors did not understand them. EIOPA suggests that complex products such as variable annuities only be sold with a financial advisor, as typical retail consumers are not likely to understand the underlying complexities of such products on their own (EIOPA, 2012).

Increasing the qualification standards for financial advisers has been another way that countries have attempted to improve the quality of financial advice provided and ensure that the advisors themselves understand the increasingly complex products which are offered. The United Kingdom, for example, has increased the educational and certification standards for its financial advisors as part of its Retail Distribution Review, with initial results showing that advisors are indeed better qualified and that the industry is becoming more professional. The Netherlands also implemented new measures to raise the qualifications needed to provide pensions advice specifically, as there were previously no clear requirements as to what capability level the advisor needed to have to give advice, and the law required a relatively low level. Subsequent review of the advice files has shown that the quality of advice has improved, though this is also likely due to other measures taken to regulate the compensation of advisors. The United States imposes additional licensing requirements such as ongoing exams and background checks, and requires training specifically on annuity products for advisors selling annuities. In Australia financial advisors and those who sell financial products must now have a specific license issued by the government. Industry bodies have also taken voluntary initiatives to increase the educational standards of its advisors, as the German Insurance Association has done in setting continued professional development standards for insurance intermediaries.

Finally, measures have been taken to make sure that the consumer is sure of their purchase by allowing for a cooling down period for consumers to be able to consider whether they made the right decision in purchasing the annuity product. Insurance regulators in the United States require that insurance companies provide a 'free look period', which allows consumers to change their mind regarding the purchase of an annuity product within a certain period of time. These types of measures can help to mitigate any negative effects from high pressure sales resulting in the purchase of an annuity product which was not suitable for the client.

The appropriate measures which policy makers should take to regulate intermediaries and ensure the quality and suitability of financial advice will depend on specific market structures and the observed issues or market failures which regulation is intending to address. The outcome of any such measure should be to ensure that consumers have access to annuity products and advice which will meet their needs.

Product disclosure

The increasing complexity of annuity products also presents a challenge to ensure that the right information is conveyed and that the products' features, risks and costs are communicated in a comprehensible and comparable manner.[5] Much of the focus of regulation with respect to consumer protection for insurance products has been to ensure that all relevant information be disclosed (OECD, 2008). However, if more complex products also result in complex product disclosure, consumers face the risk of getting lost in the paperwork and making poor decisions because they don't understand the characteristics of the products or the risks they would assume. Policy makers should therefore not only be concerned that all relevant information is included in product disclosure, but also with how it is included.

The first issue to be addressed is what information should be included in disclosures. Ideally, standardised metrics and disclosure statements would be provided to facilitate comparability across products. Some jurisdictions stipulate the minimum information that needs to be disclosed for annuity products, for example the NAIC Annuity Disclosure Model Regulation in the United States, which also stipulates that consumers be provided with a standard buyer's guide developed by the NAIC. However, the wide variety of annuity products and guarantees available makes development of standardised disclosure requirements and metrics challenging. Disclosures need to reasonably adapt to individual product characteristics. There has been some effort to standardise the types of information provided for different categories of products. The American Council of Life Insurers has developed separate standardised templates for fixed, indexed, and variable annuities and EIOPA has issued guidance on the product disclosures for variable annuity products (American Council of Life Insurers, 2010) (EIOPA, 2012). The main categories of information suggested to be included in product disclosures includes the product's features, risks, charges, and tax obligations.

In addition to providing guidance on what information to include, regulators are increasingly focusing on making sure consumers understand the product communications they receive and how to make communication regarding the product features, risks and costs more effective. For example, the Office of Information and Regulatory Affairs in the United States issued a memorandum in 2010 on Disclosure and Simplification as Regulatory Tools. The NAIC also conducted a study in 2005 to examine consumer knowledge of disclosure statements and ways to increase their effectiveness. EIOPA has issued a report on good practices for disclosing information to consumers and how to make it effective which draws heavily on behavioural insights (EIOPA, 2013). The European Union Packaged Retail and Insurance-based Investment Products (PRIIP) Regulation requires that providers of annuity products for which the income can fluctuate provide a Key Information Document (KID) to allow consumers to better understand and compare product information. The regulation defines the type of information which needs to be included in the KID and provides a template for the layout. In 2015 the Financial Conduct Authority in the United Kingdom published a discussion paper to address how to make sure product communications are effective, and commissioned Oxera to undertake a literature review on product disclosure.

Key product features should be highlighted in disclosure documents in a simple and comparable manner in line with the product's goals. Presenting information regarding the guaranteed return as opposed to the guaranteed income, for example, could undermine the goal of the annuity product to insure consumption for the consumer. Generally speaking, for many annuity products the goal is to provide protection against longevity risk, or the risk that consumers will outlive their assets in retirement. The language used to describe their guarantee should therefore be framed as such. Numerous studies have shown that consumers' preferences for annuity products are significantly influenced by the way the product is presented. Emphasising the product's ability to ensure future consumption increases the preference for annuity products, whereas emphasising the potential returns and investment outcomes decrease this preference (Agnew et al., 2008; Brown et al., 2008). Similarly, presenting a breakeven analysis of annuity products having different guarantees could misrepresent the value that the product offers. An inflation indexed annuity, for example, could present a longer time horizon to break even compared to a level payment annuity product, yet the inflation indexed annuity provides additional value in terms of purchasing power protection. Therefore a breakeven investment analysis of annuity products is not an appropriate metric to highlight the insurance benefits annuity products can offer. The main feature highlighted should therefore be the guaranteed or expected level of income that the product will provide.

Communicating the importance of certain features in clear way can also help the consumer to understand the value they provide. The value consumers place on inflation linked annuities providing purchasing power protection, for example, can be influenced by how this guarantee is communicated to consumers. These types of annuities remain extremely unpopular and protection against inflation risk largely undervalued, despite most people stating a preference for non-decreasing levels of real annuity payments. Explaining the effects of inflation on purchasing power can help consumers understand inflation risk and in turn can influence the preference for inflation linked annuities compared to level payment annuities (Beshears et al., 2012). Expressing the annual increases as an absolute value rather than a percentage also increases the consumers' value of inflation protection (Shu, Zeithammer and Payne, 2014).

Communicating the risks presented by an annuity product in a simple and understandable way is particularly challenging, as consumers' demonstrated preferences can be highly sensitive to the way in which the risk is illustrated, particularly for individuals with lower numeracy (Bateman, et al., 2011). Conveying risk is especially important for variable payment annuity products and retirement savings with a guaranteed income option, as the payments from these products can change over time and are not necessarily fully guaranteed. For these products, the potential for consumer's payments to be lower than expected or planned for needs to be highlighted in the product disclosure.

Product disclosure should therefore convey not only the expected payments from the annuity product where payments can be variable, but also the risk of any negative outcome which they could be exposed to in the event of low profits or poor market performance.

This communication should be done with care, however, given the sensitivity of preferences to the communication of risk. Individuals have a hard time interpreting probabilities, so communicating these scenarios in probabilistic terms is not ideal. Rather categorical labels have been shown to be better understood by consumers (Loewenstein et al., 2013). Therefore labelling a poor outcome as the 'worst-case scenario' or 'negative scenario' would be more effective at communicating the risk than labelling it as a percentile of a distribution of outcomes. The US Annuity Disclosure Model Regulation for example requires that both a 'low' and a 'high' scenario be illustrated. Where annuity products offer a variable annuity payment on top of a minimum guaranteed payment, the worst case scenario of only receiving the guaranteed payment should be communicated along with the expected average payment including both the guaranteed and variable portions.

Providing the expected level of annuity income for each risk scenario (worst-case, expected case etc.) in a tabular format may lead to more prudent decisions by the consumer. Some evidence has shown that illustrations of risk result in higher risk-taking than communicating the same information in textual format (Bateman, et al., 2011).

Restraint should also be used regarding the number of risk scenarios presented. Consumers tend to be overly optimistic, putting more weight on positive outcomes than on negative ones, so providing a range of scenarios tends to result in preferences for products presenting more risk (Bateman, et al., 2011).

All costs and fees for annuity products should be fully and accurately disclosed. However, while the breakdown of fees should be provided, the total upfront cost for the product and all optional add-ons should be included in the headline price. This is because consumers tend to focus primarily on the headline price, and are more susceptible to opting for extra add-ons which increase the total price in relatively small increments. Being able to compare the total upfront cost for different variations of the product facilitates the cost comparison for the consumer. In the case of fixed payment annuities, this 'cost' can also be communicated as the guaranteed income provided to the consumer for a given premium amount. For example, the additional cost of a life annuity with a guaranteed period should be included in the total price, or guaranteed income, communicated rather than as an additional fee which would be charged. The Financial Conduct Authority in the United Kingdom found that the total price for annuity products were generally communicated in this way, but that products having a drawdown element did not always effectively communicate the total costs which would be incurred (Financial Conduct Authority, 2015).

Where fees are charged on a regular basis, as is the case for example with the optional guarantees included in variable annuities, communicating the total cost of these additional options is less obvious. This complication is compounded by consumers' difficulty in processing percentages and translating percentages into meaningful information. This could be remedied by providing personalised fee information and translating the fee percentages into absolute values based on the premium the consumer is planning to pay. Expected annual costs could then be calculated in absolute terms to facilitate the consumers' comparison of how much they can expect to regularly pay for the different product options available. Consumers could then, for example, compare the total annual cost for purchasing a GMIB option compared to a GLWB option for a variable annuity product.

Irregular fees which could be incurred at some future point in time should also be disclosed not only at the time of purchase but also at the time they are incurred. For example, charges could be incurred when consumers change their investment option or decide to make withdrawals or surrender their product. Consumers are not likely to easily recall these extra charges which were communicated to them at the onset of the contract, and should be reminded when their actions will result in additional fees or impact the value of the product's guarantee. They should be required to confirm their desire to continue with their chosen action following the reminder that it will incur a charge in order to make sure that they are aware of the consequences. For example, for a retirement savings product with a guaranteed income option, consumers should be warned that a withdrawal in excess of the limit could result in an additional charge or reduction in the value of their guarantee.

Testing different formats of disclosure for specific products and environments can be an efficient way to ensure that disclosures are effective in getting the necessary information across to consumers. While the principles discussed here are expected to increase the effectiveness of product communication based on existing findings, consumer understanding is influenced by a number of other variables which could come into play. Different consumer segments may have different levels of numeracy and financial literacy, and particular product features or even the median of communication can play a significant role in how consumers understand the information that they are presented. Disclosures should therefore be tested in the environment that they are expected to be used in order to ensure that they are effective in conveying information on the product's features, risks and costs.

The potential role of technology

There is a great potential for technology to play a larger role in facilitating consumers' awareness, access and understanding of annuity products. Platforms such as the SCOMP in Chile have shown that that technology can play a central role in promoting awareness and understanding of the different options individuals have to finance their retirement. The Money Advice Service in the United Kingdom proposes enhanced annuities to consumers indicating health problems, making them aware of this option even if they previously had not been.

Technology could also be used present different annuity options side-by side in an unbiased manner, offering a potential solution to address the conflicts of interest for financial advisors. Information can furthermore be personalised to the needs and resources of the individual consumer. For example, fixed payment annuities could be proposed to individuals having a lower risk tolerance to prevent these consumers from being misled by nuances in the presentation of risk. Costs and fees could be presented in total amounts and in absolute values based on the premium that the consumer is willing to pay.

Nevertheless, given the wide array of products available and the options they offer to consumers, there will certainly be a continued need for tailored, professional advice. Policy makers should therefore encourage and facilitate the expanding role of technology in serving consumers for their decisions of how to finance their retirement while also considering other measures to ensure that retirement financial advice promotes products which best serve consumers' needs.

The following chapter will consider all of the issues raised in the previous chapters and conclude with a discussion of the considerations that policy makers should have in mind when considering the role of annuity products within the retirement landscape and implementing policies to support them.

Notes

1. In line with Principle 5 of the G20 High Level Principles on Financial Consumer Protection on Financial Education and Awareness which states that consumers should be assisted to 'take effective action to improve their own financial well-being".
2. In line with Principle 10 of the G20 High Level Principles on Financial Consumer Protection on Competition which states that consumers should be able to compare different products.
3. See OECD Pensions Outlook 2016, Chapter 3 for a more detailed discussion of these measures.
4. In line with Principle 6 of the G20 High Level Principles on Financial Consumer Protection on Responsible Business Conduct which says that financial service providers should act in the best interests of their clients and should be properly qualified, that conflicts of interest should be disclosed, and that remuneration should be designed to encourage responsible business conduct.
5. In line with Principle 4 of the G20 High Level Principles on Financial Consumer Protection on Disclosure and Transparency which states that all information should be "accurate, honest, understandable and not misleading".

References

Agarwal, S., J. C. Driscoll, X. Gabaix, D. Laibson (2009), "The Age of Reason: Financial Decisions over the Life-Cycle with Implications for Regulation".

Agnew, J. R., L. R. Anderson, J. R. Gerlach, L. R. Szykman (2008), "The Annuity Puzzle and Negative Framing", *Brief, Center for Retirement Research*, Boston.

American Council of Life Insurers (2010), "Improving Annuity Disclosure: A Life Insurance Industry Initiative".

Bateman, H., C. Eckert, J. Geweke, J. Louviere, S. Satchell, S. Thorp (2011), "Financial competence, risk presentation and retirement portfolio preferences" *Research Paper No. 2011ACTL03*, Australian School of Business.

Beshears, J., J. J. Choi, D. Laibson, B. C. Madiran, S. P. Zeldes, (2012), "What makes annuitization more appealing?" *NBER Working Paper 18575.*

Cannon, E. S., I. Tonks (2010), "Compulsory and Voluntary Annuities Markets in the UK".

Cannon, E., R. Stevens, I. Tonks, I (2013) "Price Efficiency in the Dutch Annuity Market" *Netspar Discussion Paper.*

Christoffersen, S. K., R. B. Evans, D. K. Musto, (2012), "What do Consumers' Fund Flows Maximize? Evidence from Their Brokers' Incentives".

EIOPA (2012), "Report on Good Practices for Disclosure and Selling of Variable Annuities".

EIOPA (2013), "Good practices on information provision for DC schemes: Enabling occupational DC scheme members to plan for retirement".

Federal Trade Commission (2004), "The effect of mortgage broker compensation disclosures on consumers and competition: A controlled experiment", Bureau of Economics staff report.

Financial Conduct Authority (2014), "Thematic Review of Annuities".

Financial Conduct Authority (2015), "Retirement income market study: Final report – confirmed findings and remedies".

Fong, J. H., Lemaire, J., & Tse, Y. K. (2011), "Improving Money's Worth Ratio Calculations: The Case of Singapore's Pension Annuities".

G20/OECD Task Force on Financial Consumer Protection. (2011). G20 High-Level Principles on Financial Consumer Protection, Paris. *www.oecd.org/daf/fin/financial-markets/48892010.pdf.*

G20/OECD Task Force on Financial Consumer Protection. (2013). Update Report on the Work to Support the Implementation of the G20 High-Level Principles on Financial Consumer Protection. Paris. *http://www.oecd.org/daf/fin/financial-education/G20EffectiveApproachesFCP.pdf*

G20/OECD Task Force on Financial Consumer Protection. (2014). Effective Approaches to Support the Implementation of the Remaining G20/OECD High-Level Principles on Financial Consumer Protection. Paris. *http://www.oecd.org/daf/fin/financial-education/G20-OECD-Financial-Consumer-Protection-Principles-Implementation-2014.pdf.*

Hackethal, A., R. Inderst, S Meyer (2012), "Trading on Advice".

Hung, A. A., M. Gong, J. Burke (2015), "Effective Disclosures in Financial Decisionmaking", RAND Corporation.

Lowenstein, G., C. R. Sunstein, R. Golman, (2013), "Disclosure: Psychology Changes Everything".

Milevsky, M. A., L. W. Shao (2010), "Annuities and their Derivatives: The Recent Canadian Experience" *Pension Research Council Working Paper No. 2010-16.*

Mitchell, O. S., J. Ruiz (2009), "Pension Payouts in Chile: Past, Present and Future Prospects", Population Aging Research Center Working Paper.

Mitchell, O. S., J. M. Poterba, M. J. Warshawsky, J. R. Brown (1999), "New Evidence on the Money's Worth of Individual Annuities", *The American Economic Review.*

Mullainathan, S., M. Noth, A. Schoar (2011), "The Market for Financial Advice: An Audit Study".

OECD (2008), *Improving Financial Education and Awareness on Insurance and Private Pensions*, OECD Publishing, Paris. *http://dx.doi.org/10.1787/9789264046399-en*

Oxera (2014), "Review of literature on product disclosure".

Shu, S. B., R. Zeithammer, J. Payne (2014), "Consumer Preferences for Annuities: Beyond NPV".

Stanko, D., N. Paklina (2014), "Supervising the Distribution of Annuities and other Forms of Pension Pay-Out", *IOPS Working Papers on Effective Pensions Supervision, No.21.*

Superintendencia de Pensiones. (2015). *Boletín Estadístico Electrónico N° 219.* Santiago.

von Gaudecker, H.-M., C. Weber (2004), "Surprises in a Growing Market Niche: An Evaluation of the German Private Life Annuities Market", *The Geneva Papers on Risk and Insurance,* 29(3), 394-416.

Chapter 6

Policy considerations with respect to annuity products

The policy considerations put forward in this chapter draw from the information presented in previous chapters, and are structured around four main themes: defining a common language, designing a coherent framework, keeping up with innovation and finally encouraging the risk management of annuity products.

The wide range of annuity products which are now available present new possibilities as to how these types of products can be used as a part of the retirement financing strategy of individuals. However, they also present challenges to policy makers to ensure that appropriate policies are in place to further the expected role of annuities in the retirement landscape and support the sustainability of these products, as well as to make sure that the features of these products are understood by consumers.

The issues presented in the previous chapters lead to several conclusions which policy makers should consider to support the expected role of annuity products. First, there is a need for consistency in the language used to discuss annuity products in order to establish the scope of this discussion. There is also a need for coherence in the design of the framework for the retirement landscape in order to further the expected role of annuity products to finance retirement. Continued innovation in product design highlights the need for regulatory requirements to be flexible and able to adapt to future changes, but also the need for consumers and their financial advisors to be able to understand the more complicated product features which are resulting. New risks presented by these products also require that the annuity providers manage these risks, and policies need to provide the appropriate incentives to mitigate these risks where necessary in order to ensure the sustainability of these products.

Defining a common language

The current lack of consistency with respect to the language used to discuss annuity products presents a large barrier for cross country comparison of annuity markets and products and any discussion around their use within the retirement system. In order to be able to compare annuity products and markets, the scope must be laid out, the concept clearly defined, and the terminology used to describe products and their features standardised. Deciding upon these aspects will also provide a common language with which to discuss the role that annuity products play in providing income in retirement across jurisdictions and how policy makers can support this role.

First, the scope must to be defined and the distinction made between annuity income and annuity products. Policy makers often refer to a target level of 'annuitisation' for individuals in retirement, in other words the appropriate proportion of available income in retirement which should be guaranteed. However this proportion can also potentially include income received from public pensions and income received from defined benefit pensions in addition to income received from annuity products. Therefore in order to assess the role annuity products play in providing retirement income, these different components of the overall level of annuitisation must be separated out, and the scope of what constitutes an annuity product defined. This could be done by excluding products which are not fully financed by the premium or which are not priced on an actuarially fair basis.

Secondly, the definition of an annuity product must be clear in order to distinguish these products from pension savings products which may not provide for income in retirement and from other drawdown products which provide no guarantees. This is necessary in order to assess the role of the income guarantees that annuity products offer compared to other types of pension and retirement products. This could be done by excluding products which do not provide a longevity insurance component and clarifying the definition with respect to deferred savings products which include the option or mandate to be converted into annuity income at a future date.

Finally, a common terminology is necessary to be able to first understand the features and risks of annuity products and secondly to discuss the role of policy in supporting these products. This issue is a particular problem, for example, when it comes to variable annuity products. The term 'variable annuity' is commonly applied to both variable annuity products as classified here as well as to variable payout annuities. Therefore two policy makers from different jurisdictions or organizations can find themselves discussing the challenges and risks for 'variable annuities', yet actually be referring to two different products with completely different risk profiles; the former which exposes the annuity provider to more risk, and the latter where the risk is shared with the individual. Therefore policy makers need to find a common language in order to be able to have coherent discussions with respect to the risks presented by the products and the role of policy to ensure their sustainability.

A common scope and terminology would also aid in guiding data collection efforts so as to be able to compare the size and trends of annuity markets across jurisdictions. There is currently no common standard for classifying annuity products, which also makes it difficult to understand the relative importance of the different types of annuity products across jurisdictions. Harmonising this language could also lead to a common standard for collecting and reporting data on annuity markets. However, the variables collected also need to be more comprehensive. For example it would be very useful to have data on the rate at which deferred products with an annuity option are actually converted into an income stream in order to have a clearer view on consumer preferences and how these products are used in practice.

Once a common scope and language has been agreed upon, policy makers will better be able to define clear objectives with respect to the desired role of annuity products within the retirement landscape and implement policies to support this role.

Designing a coherent framework for retirement

Policy makers need to consider numerous elements in designing the framework to support the desired role of annuities within the retirement landscape. This first involves considering how the pension system in place can accommodate annuity products. Limits on product design and pricing may also be considered in light of the needs of individuals and the risks they face for their retirement. Encouraging the demand for annuity products can also be a challenge, and policy makers must consider the most efficient way to do so given the potentially heterogeneous needs of the population.

Policy makers first need to identify where annuities should play a role in the retirement system by considering the existing pension gap and the risks that individuals will have to bear, particularly given the shift towards more individual responsibility which is occurring in many jurisdictions. The risks faced will determine the types of guarantees and flexibilities which annuities could provide to add value and increased security for the individual.

Protection from longevity risk may be most important for the payout phase, though some flexibility and liquidity may also be needed to cover unexpected expenses. Minimum return guarantees may be important particularly during the accumulation phase to protect the individual from the timing risk of retiring following a market downturn.

The rules relating to the accumulation and drawdown of pension savings need to accommodate the products which can fulfil the needs identified. For example, plan sponsors can be reluctant to make annuity products available within their plans due to duty of care requirements which could lead to legal action against the sponsor if the plan member feels the annuity product was not appropriate. This was found to be an issue in Canada and the United States. Such requirements therefore need to be clearly defined particularly with respect to annuity products to avoid ambiguities as to whether the plan sponsor has fulfilled its responsibilities towards its members.

Another consideration is any minimum or maximum distribution limit imposed. These limits need to allow for the appropriate use of annuity products to manage investment and/ or longevity risk. For example, the United States recently modified its regulation around minimum distribution limits to accommodate the use of advanced life deferred annuities to insure against longevity risk.

Limits on product features or design could potentially be considered where it is in the consumers' best interest and where the consumer may otherwise be less likely to protect themselves from the risk in question. One example could be requiring that married individuals be offered joint annuities, as is the case in Chile, in order to ensure that the surviving spouse will continue to receive income even after the death of their partner. Individuals may be less likely to choose a joint annuity on their own either due to a lack of awareness of the option or because it reduces the guaranteed income level. Another restriction could be to limit the guaranteed payment period, a feature generally preferred by consumers but which also limits the benefit of longevity risk pooling that annuities can offer. A ten year limit on the guarantee period was previously imposed in the United Kingdom.

Limits on the guarantees offered may also be imposed with the objective to limit the potential risk to the annuity provider. For example, restrictions could be imposed on the age at which guaranteed annuity conversion rates can be offered, as the risk of these guarantees significantly increases with the length of the deferral period for which they are offered. Israel has imposed such limits on annuity providers. Other jurisdictions, such as Germany, impose a maximum discount rate allowed to be used to price the annuity in order to ensure that the guaranteed rate is sustainable.

Nevertheless, any limits imposed should not unduly increase the risk to the annuity provider or the cost to the consumer. For example, requiring that annuities be indexed to inflation could certainly benefit the consumer as these types of annuities are generally not preferred over level annuities due to the present-bias of consumers and a lack of foresight as to the effects of inflation on purchasing power. However, these annuities also tend to be relatively more expensive than fixed level or escalating annuities. Furthermore if inflation-linked bonds are not widely available for the annuity provider to invest in to match this liability, an accumulated concentration of exposure to inflation risk could present a solvency risk. Another example of a limit on product features could be requiring that consumers are able to change their annuity provider. Given the long-term duration of the annuity contract, it could potentially be beneficial to allow the consumer to change their mind if they are able to get a better value elsewhere. However, such flexibility also increases the risk to the annuity provider and therefore the cost to the consumer. Transaction costs for the consumer could also be expected to increase. Alternative policy measures should therefore be considered if the objective is to encourage annuity providers to offer competitive rates.

Any limits with respect to market segmentation for pricing annuity products should be implemented with caution, particularly where the purchase of an annuity is voluntary. Such restrictions can potentially result in certain subgroups of the population being excluded from the annuity market due to anti-selection, where only consumers having higher life expectancies will purchase annuities. The most prevalent restriction on market segmentation is the restriction on gender-based pricing, as is the case in Europe. This increases the price of annuities for males, who could then decide that annuities are then too expensive given their life expectancy and drop out of the market. Eventually this could result in the price for all annuities converging to the price based on female mortality, eroding any intended benefits. On the other hand, if regulation does not allow the annuity provider to adjust its mortality assumptions to reflect the actual mortality experience, the annuity provider could face solvency problems as the premiums paid would not be sufficient to cover the liability owed.

Experience in the United Kingdom has shown that market segmentation can be beneficial to consumers in some cases. Enhanced annuities, widely available in the United Kingdom, offer higher incomes to individuals having health or lifestyle conditions which reduce their life expectancy. This product provides a solution to a population sub-group who would otherwise have been penalised from the purchase of a regular annuity.

Any mandate for the purchase of an annuity should be considered with caution, as the need for the protection that annuities can offer is likely to differ significantly across socioeconomic groups. A one-size-fits-all approach may therefore not be appropriate. This would likely penalise the lower income groups who would likely not have saved enough to purchase a meaningful level of income. It could also result in over-annuitisation of assets for other groups who need to maintain some flexibility and liquidity from their assets. These issues could partially be addressed by allowing more flexibility to withdraw accumulated assets when they do not meet or when they exceed certain thresholds.

Nevertheless, making the purchase of an annuity mandatory can be effective at increasing the demand for annuity products, and can also help to spur innovation from annuity providers looking to gain market share. This was seen to be the case in the United Kingdom which previously required that a portion of assets accumulated in defined contribution pension plans be used to purchase a life annuity. The United Kingdom now has one of the largest annuity markets, and competition for market share has resulted in the prevalence of enhanced annuities. However, given the sharp reduction in the purchase of annuities following the recent pension reforms which removed this requirement, it also presents a case study on the challenge of encouraging consumer demand for annuity products, particularly where these products are perceived as a poor value.

As an alternative to a hard mandate, policies are increasingly being used in the retirement landscape to 'nudge' consumers towards the desired behaviour, namely with automatic enrolment to save for retirement and default investment strategies. This mechanism in particular relies on the inertia of individuals to go with the 'default' option. These types of policies have been effective and useful for getting people to save during the accumulation phase. However, they need to be designed very carefully if applied for the purchase of an annuity in the decumulation phase. Experience in the United Kingdom presents evidence that providing a 'default' annuity option, in this case the annuity provided by the individual's existing pension provider, resulted in consumer apathy and a disengagement from the process, and often resulted in consumers not getting the best product available to them. Furthermore, this tendency resulted in a lack of competitive pressure on annuity providers leading to lower value product for consumers. Low-cost centralised default annuity providers could potentially be introduced to maintain competitive pressure among annuity providers. In Sweden, for example, the state Premium Pension Authority is responsible for providing the annuity. In Singapore, the Central Provident Fund provides a low-cost annuity option to compete with private annuity providers.

Rather than offering consumers the option to opt-out of a default, another approach is to make consumers actively compare products and make a choice. This approach seems to be effective at increasing engagement in the decision as well as competitive incentives for annuity providers. For example, once individuals have indicated that they plan to retire in Chile, the pension fund transmits their information to an electronic platform (the SCOMP) which then provides consumers comparable information regarding their options to take a programmed withdrawal from a pension fund or take a life annuity from an insurance company. The individual is therefore forced to choose an option, making them much less prone to the effects of inertia and staying with their current pension provider, and encouraging them to actively consider the option to purchase an annuity.

More traditional fiscal incentives can also be used to encourage individuals to purchase annuity products. These types of incentives have proven to be effective in influencing consumer's choice of annuity products in several markets, such as Denmark, Korea and the United States.

Keeping up with innovation: Ensuring sustainable and suitable annuity products

Product innovations by annuity providers may be part of the solution to encourage demand for annuity products. Much of these innovations have involved increasing the flexibility offered by the product or increasing its perceived value through risk-sharing. However policy makers must have a framework in place to keep up with these innovations and ensure that the products remain sustainable for the annuity provider and suitable for the consumer.

Product innovations involving more flexibility and risk-sharing have led to increasingly complex annuity products. Increased flexibility in particular introduces additional risk for the annuity provider which needs to be provisioned for, and reserving and capital requirements which can adapt to new product features are needed in order to ensure that the products are sustainable. Increased risk sharing, on the other hand, highlights the importance of ensuring that consumers themselves are able to understand the products they purchase and the costs and risks that they entail in order to select the most suitable product for their needs. Given product complexity, consumers may also need to rely on financial advice therefore this advice should also lead to a suitable recommendation for the consumer.

The evolution in the design and features of annuity products and the new risks which they present has made clear the need for capital requirements to be more flexible and comprehensive in the risks which are accounted for in these requirements. The increasingly dynamic nature of annuity products and their guarantees requires reserve and solvency capital requirements that are also more dynamic in order to reflect the underlying risks and ensure sufficient assets to back the annuity providers' liabilities. Static, formula-based approaches are no longer adequate for the new generations of annuity products.

Approaches based on principles for the calculation of reserve and solvency capital requirements are needed to allow for the flexibility in calculations to capture changing provisioning needs in light of innovations in annuity product design. This type of approach has been widely adopted in particular in light of the dynamic nature and risks presented by variable annuities, and allows for the use of stochastic scenarios and the recognition of the behavioural risks coming from increased flexibility offered by these annuity products. Reserve and solvency calculations could also be complemented with additional stress and scenario testing to ensure that the nature of all risk exposures and the interaction of these risks is recognised and understood.

The increased complexity and dynamic nature of annuity products also presents a need to communicate product features and risks to consumers through effective product disclosures in order to ensure that consumers understand the product that they are purchasing. This disclosure needs to clearly communicate the main features of the annuity product, any risks that this product entails for the consumer and all applicable fees relating to the product's purchase and use.

Disclosure requirements should therefore also move to an approach based on principles, focusing not only on the type of information which is included but also how it is included. Regulation often stipulates the minimum information that is required to be included in annuity product disclosures, but given the constant innovation with respect to product features and guarantees, minimum requirements could quickly become insufficient. The key features highlighted and metrics used should be presented in a manner which is in line with the goals of the product and the risks it is meant to insure against. To ensure that the consumer is aware of any risks from the annuity product, disclosures should convey not only the expected payments but also the potential negative outcomes to which the consumer could be exposed to in the event of low profits or poor market performance, particularly for annuity products with risk-sharing arrangements. All costs and fees for the annuity products should be fully and accurately disclosed at the onset of the contract as well as at the time at which they are incurred. The effectiveness of product disclosures may vary with the type of product, the context and the median with which the information is presented. Disclosures should therefore be tested for effectiveness in the context in which they will be used in order to ensure that the targeted consumers do indeed understand the essential information provided.

Given the increasing complexity of annuity products, the role of financial advice in helping consumers to understand the different types of products and select the product which is most suitable may also be increasing in importance. Ensuring that the financial advisor reliably and effectively communicates product features and risks to the consumer and can match these with the consumers' needs is therefore necessary. Policy makers can address this issue from several angles. First is ensuring that the advisors themselves understand the products available, secondly is ensuring that their advice is in the interest of the consumer and finally is providing the consumers with tools to better judge whether they are getting appropriate advice.

Policy makers first need to ensure that financial advisers are also keeping up with the innovation in the annuity product market and not only are aware of the products available but also have the knowledge to understand the underlying mechanisms of the product. Several jurisdictions address this through ongoing education and examination requirements for advisors to ensure that they are sufficiently trained on the products they sell and are able to make appropriate recommendations.

Various approaches can be taken to help ensure that product advice is in the interest of the consumer and that they end up with a suitable product. The most common approaches focus first on duty of care standards for financial advice and secondly on the way in which advisors are compensated for their services. First, duty of care sets a standard for the advice itself, but the way in which it is defined and enforced can vary. At one end of the spectrum, it can be defined as a strict legal standard such as fiduciary duty, which offers legal recourse to the affected consumer in the event that the product was not in their best interest. Less stringent standards, however, require only a determination of whether the product is reasonably suitable for the consumer.

Regulation of compensation structures, on the other hand, aims directly to mitigate any potential conflicts of interest for the advisor which could inadvertently or otherwise result in less suitable advice for the consumer. Measures taken to address this issue can vary from banning commissions completely, banning certain commission structures or imposing a cap on the commission. However, while such measures may help to improve the quality of financial advice by better aligning the interests of the advisor and the consumer, there is a risk that such limits could lead to a reduced take-up of financial advice. The costs and benefits should therefore be carefully weighted when considering limits on compensation, and the appropriate measure to take will depend on the particular problems observed in the market.[1]

Finally policy makers can try to provide consumers with the tools with which to assess the advice received. This is most often done through the required disclosure of commissions paid to the advisor. Nevertheless some evidence indicates that consumers do not use and act on this information to assess any potential incentives to recommend one course of action over another or call into question the advice they receive, so this measure alone is not likely to be effective. Another tool is the cooling-off period implemented in some jurisdictions, which allows the consumer time to digest the advice and product information and change their mind regarding their purchase. Nevertheless the effectiveness of this measure also relies on the quality and clarity of the product disclosure and information provided.

Encouraging appropriate risk management

Ensuring the sustainability and suitability of products in the evolving annuities landscape also involves ensuring that the risks resulting from these products are able to be managed appropriately by the annuity providers. These exposures are determined by product design and the features and flexibility the products offered as well as how the market or longevity experience evolves going forward. Annuity providers need to ensure that they will be able to make the payments promised to annuitants, even in the event where experience deviate from expectations, for example lower than expected investment returns. The framework that policy makers put in place must therefore also encourage annuity providers to have a clear view of their risk exposures and mitigate the risk where needed, incentivising the appropriate risk management of annuity products through the accounting framework, investment limits and the capital requirements which are in place.

Policy makers need to be aware of the potential impact that accounting standards can have on the risk exposures from the different types of annuity products in order to identify any potential misalignment of risk management incentives or areas which may need additional monitoring. For example, the accounting framework will directly affect the risk exposures from participating annuity products in particular, as the calculation of the surplus to be shared with the annuitants will depend on the accounting measure used.

Historical valuation methods will result in more balance sheet stability, as unrealised gains and losses are not recognised and therefore would not be shared with the annuitant. On the other hand, fair value methods which better reflect the financial position of the entity will result in higher levels of volatility both for the annuity provider's balance sheet as well as for the payments to the annuitant. To manage this potential volatility and reduce its risk exposure from an economic point of view, the annuity provider may establish a buffer reserve to smooth payments to the annuitant by retaining some of the profits during good periods to be paid out during less profitable periods. However, supervisors need to closely monitor and understand the calculations underlying such smoothing mechanisms in order to ensure fairness and transparency of the profit participation. Furthermore, any minimum participation rate imposed by regulation must take into account the interaction between the participation rate, the accounting measure and any smoothing mechanism imposed to ensure that the annuity provider is able to manage the resulting volatility exposure and solvency risk.

The accounting framework can also have an impact on the risk management strategy implemented for annuity products where dynamic hedging strategies for market risks are used, such as with variable annuities. Such strategies rely on the measurement of the annuity liability value at a given point in time, which is determined by the accounting measure used. Dynamic hedging strategies based on Generally Accepted Accounting Principles (GAAP) or statutory measures of the liability can result in an under-hedging of certain risks compared to hedging on an economic basis. Supervisors may therefore want to also monitor economic measures of the balance sheet so as to not provide a disincentive for annuity providers to more fully hedge their risk exposures on an economic basis.

Policy makers should also ensure that annuity providers are able to effectively use and implement appropriate strategies to mitigate their risk exposure. For example, investment in financial derivatives should be allowed where these instruments can be used to hedge risk exposures. However, supervisors should also ensure the effectiveness of such strategies. Some jurisdictions address this by requiring that annuity providers submit a plan for their use of derivatives as well as their resulting investments. This allows supervisors to ensure that these instruments are being used as part of an effective hedging strategy and not for speculative purposes, as well as to monitor annuity providers' overall exposure to derivatives.

In addition to ensuring the effectiveness of any risk mitigation strategy, policy makers should also be aware of any potential increase in risk as a result of the strategy. For example, the use of over-the-counter (OTC) derivative instruments to hedge market risks can also increase the counterparty risk exposure of the annuity provider. Such exposures are generally addressed through concentration limits to counterparty exposure. However recent regulation implemented such as the Dodd-Frank Act in the United States and the European Market Infrastructure Regulation (EMIR) in Europe have sought to reduce this risk through centralised clearing and collateral requirements. While such measures can be effective in reducing counterparty exposure, they may also increase liquidity risk or duration mismatching as a result of the collateral requirements. Therefore policy makers must find a balance so as to ensure that the overall reduction of risk results from risk mitigating measures and not reduce the incentives for annuity providers to mitigate their risk exposures.

Capital requirements, including both reserve and solvency capital requirements, should recognise the risk reduction from any risk mitigation strategies in order to serve as an incentive for annuity providers to hedge their risk exposures. This includes, for example, the recognition of reinsurance coverage as well as investment strategies which minimise the asset-liability duration gap or otherwise reduce the investment risk exposure of the annuity provider. Partial risk reduction may also be recognised, such as for dynamic hedging strategies where the hedge is approximate by nature. For example, both Canada and the United States only partially recognise the risk reduction from dynamic hedging strategies in reserve and solvency capital requirements for variable annuity products, as the effectiveness of these strategies is not expected to be perfect.

Summary of policy considerations

Annuity products and the guarantees that they offer may provide part of the solution to address the increasing investment and longevity risks that individuals are facing. Product innovations enhancing the attractiveness of these products for consumers through increased flexibility or lower cost through risk-sharing mechanisms which reduce the level of guarantees broaden the menu of options available and the ability for these products to meet the varied needs of consumers.

Nevertheless, in order for these products to provide an effective solution, policy makers must consider the challenges that these products present with respect to their underlying risks and their increasing complexity in order to ensure the sustainability of these products for annuity providers and their suitability for consumers.

The first barrier for policy makers to overcome is the lack of consistency with respect to what is meant by an annuity product and the terminology used to describe the different types of products. The definitions and classifications presented in this chapter could serve as a starting point to arrive at a common language for discussing the role of annuity products and the related policy considerations. The proposed classification could also serve as a basis for comparable data collection on the size and composition of annuity markets.

Policy makers also need to design a coherent pension framework which facilitates the expected role of annuity products to provide income in retirement. The rules around the accumulation and drawdown of pension assets need to accommodate the annuity products which can meet individuals' needs at the various stages of their retirement planning. Limits on annuity product design or features, including limits on factors used for pricing, should not be imposed without considering the impact on the cost and risk exposure of the annuity product.

Moreover, the use of annuity products needs to be encouraged. Given the heterogeneous needs of society, particularly between high and low socioeconomic groups, a one-size-fits-all prescription is not likely to be appropriate. Default options can increase take-up, but need to be carefully designed so as to maintain competitive pressure among annuity providers. The effective provision of information on the options available and engaging individuals in the decision of whether to purchase an annuity is another option. Fiscal incentives can also be a useful tool to encourage demand for annuity products.

Approaches based on principles are better suited than approaches based on static formulas to ensure that capital requirements are able to adapt to changing product features. The continued innovation in annuity product design requires the regulatory framework to be more flexible and adaptive to changing risk exposures and risk drivers in order for capital requirements to remain sufficient to back the annuity liabilities and guarantee the sustainability of these products.

Policy makers also need to make sure that consumers are purchasing products which are suitable for their needs, particularly given the increased complexity of products that has accompanied innovation. Product disclosures should not only provide a minimum level of information regarding the product features, risks and costs, but also ensure that this information is easy for the consumer to understand. Policy makers can help to make sure that financial advice for these products is suitable through qualification and education requirements for advisors, duty of care standards or potentially limits on compensation structures. Commission disclosure requirements and cooling-off periods can also provide the consumer with tools to better assess the quality of the advice they receive.

Finally, the regulatory framework should ensure that the tools to manage risk and the incentives to do so are in place in order to encourage appropriate risk management by annuity providers. Supervisors should ensure that the relevant accounting measures are monitored to ensure a realistic view of risk exposures and to provide an incentive to manage risks effectively. Hedging should be facilitated, but the strategies should be monitored to ensure their effectiveness in reducing overall risk exposures. Any requirements to control the risks from the strategies themselves should also ensure that overall risk reduction still results, so as to avoid reducing incentives to hedge. Finally, capital requirements should reflect the reduction of risk from any effective risk mitigation measures in order to align with the incentives of annuity providers to manage their risk exposures.

Implementing effective policy to support the annuity products to finance retirement requires that the mechanisms and risks these products present be understood by all stakeholders. Annuity providers must recognise and understand the dynamics of risk to ensure that their products are sustainable, consumers must understand how the products function in order to select the most suitable, and policy makers need to be able to monitor the risks to ensure the continued relevancy of the regulatory framework in place. As such, the framework put in place should be designed to keep up with innovation and adapt to the changing retirement landscape.

Note

1. See OECD Pension Outlook 2016, Chapter 3.

Glossary

Accumulation phase – for a deferred annuity, the time between the purchase of the annuity product and the period when annuity payments or withdrawals begin

ALDA – An advanced life deferred annuity, which is an annuity purchased at or around retirement age, with payments deferred to begin at least ten years into the future

Annuitisation – the conversion of a certain level of assets into a guaranteed income stream

Annuity certain – annuity whose number of payments is fixed at issue (e.g. payments for 10 years)

Deferred annuity – annuity which begins payments at some point in the future after purchase

Enhanced annuity – annuity which guarantees higher payments to individuals having a lower life expectancy

Fixed indexed annuity – a retirements savings product with a guaranteed income option which allows the individual to choose among several guaranteed return or index funds with capped participation on index returns, protection from market downturns and an option to convert accumulated assets into a guaranteed income stream at some point in the future at a fixed annuity conversion rate

Fixed payment annuity – annuity whose guaranteed payments are defined in advance

Fund switching - option of the annuitant to change the investment strategy of the underlying assets

Group annuity – annuity which is not purchased for an individual, but a group of individuals (e.g. an annuity bought by an employer to cover all employees).

Guaranteed annuity conversion rate – rate of conversion of accumulated funds into an annuity at a future point in time (e.g. Guaranteed Annuity Option), effectively locking in the discount rate and mortality used to value the annuity

Immediate annuity – annuities which begin payments immediately at the end of the period at which the annuity was bought (e.g. payments begin at the end of the month)

Indexed payment annuity – annuity whose payments vary according to an independent and objective measure which is regularly computed (e.g. inflation linked, participating annuities depending on company's profits)

Individual annuity – annuities which are purchased by individuals (including joint and survivor annuities)

Inflation linked annuity – annuity whose payments are indexed to a measure of inflation

Joint annuity – annuity whose payments are contingent on the survival of two lives

Life annuity – annuity whose payments continue until the annuitant's death, providing to the annuitant protection from outliving one's financial resources (longevity risk)

GLWB – Guaranteed Minimum Lifetime Withdrawal Benefit that guarantees a minimum level of withdrawals, typically defined as a percentage of the guarantee level, which in some cases has the potential to continue to increase in the event that the account value grows. This benefit allows continued participation in market returns during the drawdown phase without requiring full annuitisation, and guarantees withdrawals for life even if the account value falls to zero.

GMAB – Guaranteed minimum accumulation benefit which guarantees a minimum return on assets for the purpose of taking a lump sum withdrawal from the product at a specified future date; the amount paid will be the maximum of the actual account value or the guaranteed value.

GMDB – Guaranteed minimum death benefit which guarantees a minimum sum to be paid to beneficiaries upon death; the amount paid will be the maximum of the actual account value or the guaranteed value.

GMIB – Guaranteed minimum income benefit which guarantees a minimum rate of return on investment during the accumulation/deferral phase for the calculation of the conversion of the accumulated funds into a fixed annuity, effectively guaranteeing a minimum level of income from the future annuity payments.

OTC – over the counter derivative contract which is privately traded in a bilateral fashion rather than being traded on a centralised exchange

Partial surrender – option of the annuitant to withdraw amounts permanently from the underlying assets, which should also typically reduce the level of any underlying guarantees

Participating annuity – annuity whose payments are indexed to the profits of the annuity provider

Payout phase – period in which annuity payments or withdrawals are taken by the annuitant

Retirement savings with guaranteed income option – deferred annuity product where the individual has some choice in how the underlying assets are invested, retains access to the underlying funds and has the option to convert the accumulated assets into a guaranteed income stream at a guaranteed annuity conversion rate at some point in the future

Surrender – option for the annuitant to terminate his contract with the provider

Timing of annuitisation/withdrawal – For a deferred annuity, the option of the annuitant to decide at what age to annuitise or begin taking guaranteed withdrawals

Variable annuity – a retirement savings product with a guaranteed income option that also offers additional guarantees such as minimum accumulation, minimum death benefit or minimum income levels

Variable payout annuity – annuity whose payments are indexed to the underlying investment performance

ORGANISATION FOR ECONOMIC CO-OPERATION AND DEVELOPMENT

The OECD is a unique forum where governments work together to address the economic, social and environmental challenges of globalisation. The OECD is also at the forefront of efforts to understand and to help governments respond to new developments and concerns, such as corporate governance, the information economy and the challenges of an ageing population. The Organisation provides a setting where governments can compare policy experiences, seek answers to common problems, identify good practice and work to co-ordinate domestic and international policies.

The OECD member countries are: Australia, Austria, Belgium, Canada, Chile, the Czech Republic, Denmark, Estonia, Finland, France, Germany, Greece, Hungary, Iceland, Ireland, Israel, Italy, Japan, Korea, Latvia, Luxembourg, Mexico, the Netherlands, New Zealand, Norway, Poland, Portugal, the Slovak Republic, Slovenia, Spain, Sweden, Switzerland, Turkey, the United Kingdom and the United States. The European Union takes part in the work of the OECD.

OECD Publishing disseminates widely the results of the Organisation's statistics gathering and research on economic, social and environmental issues, as well as the conventions, guidelines and standards agreed by its members.

OECD PUBLISHING, 2, rue André-Pascal, 75775 PARIS CEDEX 16
(21 2016 05 1P1) ISBN 978-92-64-26530-1 – 2016

www.ingramcontent.com/pod-product-compliance
Lightning Source LLC
LaVergne TN
LVHW081414110826
845149LV00010B/1744